Amazing World Facts

A Journey Through Geography and Culture

Park Windsor

Contents

Chapter 1
Introduction to Amazing World Facts

The Fascination of Discovering World Facts

Embarking on a journey through the vast expanse of our planet's geography and culture is akin to unlocking a treasure trove of wonders. From the sprawling plains of Africa to the majestic peaks of the Himalayas, and from the bustling streets of Tokyo to the serene beauty of the Amazon rainforest, our world is a tapestry woven with diversity and richness beyond compare.

What makes this journey truly captivating is the endless array of fascinating facts waiting to be unearthed. These facts are not merely pieces of information; they are windows into the intricate tapestry of human history, natural phenomena, and cultural heritage that define our world.

Consider, for instance, the Great Barrier Reef, stretching over 2,300 kilometers off the coast of Australia. This awe-inspiring ecosystem is not only the largest coral reef system on the planet but also home to an astonishing variety of marine life, making it one of the most biodiverse places on Earth.

Or take the Great Wall of China, a marvel of ancient engineering that spans over 21,000 kilometers and stands as a testament to human ingenuity and determination. Built over centuries to protect China from invaders, it is one of the most iconic structures in the world, drawing millions of visitors each year.

From the ancient wonders of the world to the modern marvels of technology, every corner of our planet holds secrets waiting to be uncovered. Whether it's the mysterious Nazca Lines in Peru, the breathtaking Northern Lights in Scandinavia, or the vibrant street markets of Marrakech, each discovery adds a new layer to our understanding of the world and its infinite wonders.

But perhaps the greatest fascination lies in the realization that, despite our differences in language, culture, and geography, we are all interconnected as inhabitants of this remarkable planet. Through the exploration of world facts, we not only expand our knowledge but also deepen our appreciation for the diversity and beauty that make our world truly extraordinary.

So let us embark on this journey together, armed with curiosity and wonder, as we uncover the amazing world facts that continue to inspire and amaze us at every turn.

The Role of Curiosity in Exploring the World

Curiosity, the insatiable thirst for knowledge and understanding, is the driving force behind our exploration of the world. It is the spark that ignites our desire to uncover the mysteries of distant lands, to unravel the secrets of ancient civilizations, and to delve into the wonders of nature.

From the moment we are born, curiosity propels us forward, compelling us to reach out, to touch, to taste, to explore. It is through curiosity that we learn to make sense of the world around us, to ask questions, and to seek answers. And as we grow, so too does our curiosity, evolving from simple wonderings to deeper inquiries that challenge our perceptions and expand our horizons.

In the realm of geography and culture, curiosity serves as our compass, guiding us on a journey of discovery across continents and centuries. It leads us to explore the towering peaks of the Himalayas, the vast deserts of Africa, and the lush rainforests of the Amazon. It drives us to immerse ourselves in the rich tapestry of human history, from the ancient civilizations of Mesopotamia and Egypt to the bustling metropolises of the modern world.

But perhaps most importantly, curiosity opens our minds to the diversity of the world and the people who inhabit it. It encourages us to embrace new experiences, to challenge our assumptions, and to celebrate the differences that make each culture unique. Through curiosity, we learn to appreciate the beauty of a traditional Japanese tea ceremony, the rhythm of a Brazilian samba, or the intricacies of a Maasai tribal dance.

In the pursuit of amazing world facts, curiosity is not merely a tool but a way of life—a constant companion that fuels our passion for exploration and discovery. It reminds us that the world is vast and boundless, filled with wonders waiting to be uncovered by those who dare to ask, "What if?" So let us embrace our curiosity, for it is the key that unlocks the door to a world of endless possibility and wonder.

The Diversity of Facts Across Continents

As we embark on our journey through the fascinating realm of world facts, one of the most striking aspects we encounter is the sheer diversity that exists across continents. From the icy expanses of Antarctica to the sun-drenched shores of the Caribbean, each corner of the globe holds its own unique tapestry of wonders waiting to be discovered.

Consider, for instance, the rich cultural heritage of Asia, home to ancient civilizations like China, India, and Japan. Here, one can marvel at the grandeur of the Taj Mahal in India, explore the intricate temples of Angkor Wat in Cambodia, or witness the serene beauty of cherry blossoms in Japan. Asia's vastness encompasses a kaleidoscope of languages, religions, and traditions, each contributing to the vibrant tapestry of its cultural landscape.

Venture across the Atlantic to the continent of Europe, and you'll encounter a treasure trove of historical landmarks, artistic masterpieces, and culinary delights. From the iconic Eiffel Tower in Paris to the majestic castles of Scotland, Europe's diverse geography and rich history offer a multitude of fascinating facts waiting to be uncovered.

Travel south to Africa, and you'll find yourself immersed in a world of breathtaking landscapes, from the sweeping savannas of the Serengeti to the towering peaks of Mount Kilimanjaro. But Africa's richness extends far beyond its natural beauty; it is also home to a wealth of cultural traditions, from the vibrant rhythms of West African music to the intricate beadwork of Maasai artisans.

Cross the Pacific to the vast continent of Australia, and you'll discover a land of contrasts, from the arid deserts of the Outback to the lush rainforests of the Daintree. Here, you can learn about the ancient Aboriginal cultures that have thrived for thousands of years, or marvel at the unique wildlife found nowhere else on Earth, such as kangaroos, koalas, and the elusive platypus.

Finally, journey to the Americas, where you'll encounter a rich tapestry of cultures spanning from the icy tundra of Alaska to the tropical rainforests of the Amazon. From the ancient ruins of Machu Picchu in Peru to the bustling streets of New York City, the Americas offer a wealth of amazing world facts that reflect the diversity and dynamism of the people who call this continent home.

The Connection Between Geography and Culture

As we delve into the realm of amazing world facts, one cannot ignore the profound connection between geography and culture. Geography, the study of the Earth's landscapes, features, and phenomena, serves as the canvas upon which the rich tapestry of human culture is woven. Indeed, the interplay between geography and culture shapes the way people live, think, and interact with their surroundings.

Consider, for instance, the impact of geography on settlement patterns and economic activities. In regions with fertile soil and ample water sources, such as the Nile River Valley in Egypt or the Ganges River Basin in India, agriculture thrives, leading to the development of complex civilizations and cultural traditions centered around farming. Similarly, coastal areas often give rise to vibrant maritime cultures, where fishing and trade play central roles in shaping the way of life.

Geography also influences the development of transportation networks and communication systems, which in turn shape cultural exchange and interaction. Mountainous terrain, for example, may hinder travel and isolate communities, leading to the development of distinct languages, customs, and traditions. Conversely, trade routes crisscrossing continents facilitate the exchange of goods, ideas, and cultural practices, fostering a rich tapestry of diversity and interconnectedness.

Moreover, geography influences the availability of natural resources, which in turn shape cultural practices and beliefs. In regions abundant in forests, such as the Amazon Basin in South America or the boreal forests of Siberia, indigenous cultures have developed deep spiritual connections to the land and its resources, often incorporating rituals and ceremonies to honor nature's bounty. Likewise, desert cultures have adapted ingenious techniques for conserving water and harnessing scarce resources, shaping their cultural identity and way of life.

But perhaps most importantly, geography shapes the way people perceive and interact with the natural world, influencing their beliefs, values, and worldview. From the reverence for mountains and rivers in Himalayan cultures to the spiritual significance of sacred groves in Celtic traditions, geography imbues the landscape with cultural meaning and significance, fostering a deep sense of connection and belonging.

The Joy of Sharing Amazing World Facts

Embarking on a journey through the fascinating realm of amazing world facts is not only a voyage of personal discovery but also an opportunity to share the joy of exploration with others. The beauty of uncovering intriguing tidbits about our planet's geography and culture lies not only in the acquisition of knowledge but in the delight of passing it along, igniting curiosity and wonder in those around us.

Imagine the excitement of sharing the remarkable fact that the Great Wall of China, stretching over 21,000 kilometers, is visible from space, or the wonder of revealing that the deepest point on Earth, the Mariana Trench, plunges to a depth of over 10,900 meters below sea level. These astonishing nuggets of information have the power to captivate imaginations and spark conversations, inviting others to join in the journey of exploration.

Moreover, sharing amazing world facts fosters a sense of connection and community, transcending geographical boundaries and cultural differences. Whether exchanging trivia with friends over coffee, engaging in lively discussions with classmates, or posting fascinating tidbits on social media, the act of sharing fosters a collective sense of wonder and appreciation for the vast diversity of our planet.

Furthermore, sharing amazing world facts serves as a gateway to deeper understanding and empathy. By learning about the cultural practices, traditions, and landmarks that shape different parts of the world, we gain insight into the rich tapestry of human experience and cultivate empathy for people whose lives may be vastly different from our own. Through the exchange of knowledge and ideas, we build bridges of understanding that transcend language and cultural barriers, fostering a more inclusive and interconnected global community.

Chapter 2
Geographic Wonders

Exploring Natural Wonders: From Grand Canyons to Northern Lights

Nature has bestowed upon our planet an abundance of breathtaking wonders, from majestic canyons to mesmerizing displays of light in the sky. These geographic marvels captivate our imagination and remind us of the awe-inspiring power and beauty of the natural world.

One of the most iconic natural wonders is the Grand Canyon, located in the state of Arizona, USA. Carved by the mighty Colorado River over millions of years, this vast chasm stretches for over 446 kilometers and reaches depths of over 1,800 meters. The Grand Canyon's sheer size and intricate rock formations, painted in hues of red, orange, and gold, make it a testament to the forces of erosion and geology that have shaped our planet over millennia.

Travel north to the Arctic regions, and you may be treated to one of nature's most breathtaking displays: the Northern Lights, also known as the Aurora Borealis. Dancing across the night sky in a mesmerizing array of colors, from shimmering greens and blues to vibrant purples and pinks, this celestial phenomenon is caused by the interaction of charged particles from the sun with the Earth's magnetic field. Witnessing the Northern Lights is an otherworldly experience that leaves observers in awe of the cosmic forces at play in our universe.

In contrast to the rugged grandeur of the Grand Canyon and the ethereal beauty of the Northern Lights, the Great Barrier Reef in Australia offers a glimpse into the vibrant underwater world that teems with life. Stretching over 2,300 kilometers along the coast of Queensland, this magnificent coral reef system is the largest of its kind on Earth and is home to an astonishing variety of marine species, from colorful fish and sea turtles to majestic manta rays and whale sharks. Snorkeling or diving in the crystal-clear waters of the Great Barrier Reef offers a unique opportunity to explore an ecosystem of unparalleled biodiversity and beauty.

Venturing further afield, the Victoria Falls, straddling the border between Zambia and Zimbabwe in southern Africa, is another natural wonder that leaves visitors spellbound. Known as "Mosi-oa-Tunya" or

"The Smoke That Thunders" in the local Tonga language, these awe-inspiring waterfalls cascade over a width of more than 1,700 meters and plunge to a depth of over 100 meters, creating a deafening roar and a misty spray that can be seen and felt for kilometers around.

Breathtaking Mountains and Their Secrets

Mountains stand as silent sentinels, towering symbols of power, resilience, and beauty. From the jagged peaks of the Himalayas to the snow-capped summits of the Andes, these majestic formations hold a wealth of secrets waiting to be uncovered.

Among the most awe-inspiring mountain ranges is the Himalayas, home to the world's highest peaks, including Mount Everest, the tallest mountain on Earth. Standing at a staggering 8,848 meters above sea level, Everest has long captured the imagination of adventurers and mountaineers, drawing them to its icy slopes in pursuit of the ultimate challenge. But beyond its towering height, the Himalayas hold a rich tapestry of cultural and ecological diversity, with ancient traditions, vibrant communities, and rare wildlife thriving amidst its rugged terrain.

In South America, the Andes stretch like a colossal spine along the western edge of the continent, encompassing a stunning array of landscapes and ecosystems. Here, one can marvel at the surreal beauty of the Atacama Desert, the world's driest desert, or explore the lush valleys and cloud forests that cradle ancient Inca ruins. The Andes are not only a geographic wonder but also a cultural treasure trove, home to indigenous peoples whose traditions and way of life have endured for millennia.

Closer to home, the Rocky Mountains of North America offer a playground for outdoor enthusiasts and nature lovers alike. Stretching from Alaska to New Mexico, these rugged peaks are a haven for wildlife, including grizzly bears, elk, and mountain goats. The Rockies also boast a rich mining history, with abandoned ghost towns and relics of the gold rush era scattered amidst their rocky slopes.

But perhaps the most intriguing aspect of mountains lies beneath their surface, hidden from view. Deep within their rocky cores, geologists uncover clues to Earth's tumultuous past, unraveling the mysteries of plate tectonics, volcanic activity, and the formation of continents. Mountains are also vital sources of freshwater, with glaciers and snowpacks feeding rivers that sustain millions of people downstream.

Yet, for all their grandeur and majesty, mountains are also fragile ecosystems facing threats from climate change, deforestation, and overdevelopment.

The Mystery of Deep Oceans and Mariana Trench

Beneath the shimmering surface of our planet's oceans lies a world of mystery and wonder, largely unexplored and teeming with secrets waiting to be revealed. At the forefront of this enigmatic realm is the Mariana Trench, the deepest known part of Earth's oceans and one of the most intriguing geographic wonders on our planet.

Located in the western Pacific Ocean, the Mariana Trench stretches over 2,550 kilometers in length and plunges to depths exceeding 10,900 meters. To put this into perspective, if Mount Everest, the tallest mountain on Earth, were placed at the bottom of the Mariana Trench, its peak would still be over 2,000 meters underwater.

The sheer depth of the Mariana Trench presents a unique set of challenges to exploration, including extreme pressure, darkness, and frigid temperatures. Yet, despite these formidable obstacles, scientists and researchers have embarked on expeditions to uncover the mysteries hidden within its depths.

One of the most astonishing discoveries made in the Mariana Trench is the existence of bizarre and otherworldly creatures adapted to survive in this extreme environment. From bioluminescent fish and translucent jellyfish to giant amphipods and elusive deep-sea squids, the Mariana Trench is home to a diverse array of marine life found nowhere else on Earth.

Moreover, the geological features of the Mariana Trench offer insights into the dynamic processes shaping our planet's surface. Subduction zones, where one tectonic plate is forced beneath another, are responsible for the formation of deep ocean trenches like the Mariana Trench. By studying these processes, scientists gain a better understanding of plate tectonics, earthquakes, and volcanic activity, which play crucial roles in shaping Earth's landscapes and ecosystems.

Despite decades of exploration, much of the Mariana Trench remains uncharted territory, with vast swathes of its depths still shrouded in mystery. New discoveries continue to astonish and inspire, fueling the imagination and driving further exploration of this remote and fascinating corner of our planet.

Islands of Intrigue: Easter Island, Galápagos, and More

Islands hold a special allure, captivating the imagination with their isolation, biodiversity, and unique cultures. Across the world, certain islands stand out as epicenters of intrigue and wonder, offering a glimpse into the complex interplay of geography, ecology, and human history. Among these islands, Easter Island and the Galápagos archipelago are particularly renowned for their fascinating landscapes, biodiversity, and cultural heritage.

Easter Island, also known as Rapa Nui, is a remote volcanic island located in the southeastern Pacific Ocean. What makes Easter Island truly remarkable are its iconic moai statues, towering stone monoliths carved centuries ago by the island's Polynesian inhabitants. These enigmatic statues, some reaching heights of over 10 meters and weighing up to 80 tons, are a testament to the ingenuity and craftsmanship of the island's ancient civilization. Yet, the mystery of Easter Island extends beyond its monumental statues, with the island's isolated location and ecological challenges sparking ongoing debate among historians, archaeologists, and anthropologists.

In contrast, the Galápagos Islands, located off the coast of Ecuador in the eastern Pacific Ocean, are renowned for their unparalleled biodiversity and unique ecosystems. Famous for inspiring Charles Darwin's theory of evolution by natural selection, the Galápagos are home to an astonishing array of wildlife found nowhere else on Earth. Giant tortoises, marine iguanas, blue-footed boobies, and Galápagos penguins are just a few of the species that inhabit these volcanic islands, each adapted to their specific island environment through millennia of isolation and evolution.

But the allure of islands extends beyond Easter Island and the Galápagos. From the tropical paradise of Bora Bora in French Polynesia to the rugged landscapes of Iceland, islands around the world offer a wealth of natural wonders, cultural treasures, and adventure opportunities waiting to be discovered. Whether exploring ancient ruins, snorkeling among vibrant coral reefs, or simply relaxing on pristine beaches, each island destination offers a unique and unforgettable experience.

The Power of Volcanoes and Ring of Fire

Volcanoes are among the most awe-inspiring natural phenomena on Earth, wielding immense power and shaping the landscapes around them. Nowhere is this more evident than in the Ring of Fire, a horseshoe-shaped region encircling the Pacific Ocean known for its volcanic activity and seismicity.

Stretching from the coasts of South America, through North America, across the Pacific to Asia, and down to Oceania, the Ring of Fire is home to around 75% of the world's active and dormant volcanoes. This vast expanse of fiery geological activity is a testament to the dynamic forces at work beneath the Earth's surface.

The volcanic activity along the Ring of Fire is driven by the movement of tectonic plates, vast slabs of the Earth's crust that float on the semi-fluid mantle beneath them. As these plates collide, subduct, or slide past one another, they create intense geological activity, including volcanic eruptions, earthquakes, and the formation of mountain ranges.

One of the most iconic volcanic peaks along the Ring of Fire is Mount Fuji, Japan's highest mountain and a symbol of national pride and cultural significance. Rising to a height of 3,776 meters, Fuji-san, as it is known in Japanese, has been revered for centuries as a sacred mountain and pilgrimage site, inspiring artists, poets, and adventurers alike.

Further south, Indonesia is home to some of the world's most active and volatile volcanoes, including Mount Merapi on the island of Java and Mount Agung on the island of Bali. These towering peaks loom large in the cultural and spiritual life of the Indonesian people, who have learned to coexist with the ever-present threat of volcanic activity.

But while volcanoes are often associated with destruction and danger, they also play a vital role in shaping the Earth's surface and supporting diverse ecosystems. Volcanic soil is rich in nutrients, making it ideal for agriculture, while volcanic islands provide habitats for unique flora and fauna found nowhere else on Earth.

Chapter 3
Unique Countries and Borders

Micro-Nations and Enclaves: The World's Smallest Countries

While large and populous countries often dominate global headlines, there exists a fascinating world of tiny nations, micro-nations, and enclaves scattered across the globe. Despite their small size, these countries boast unique cultures, histories, and identities, offering a glimpse into the diversity of human civilization.

One of the most famous micro-nations is Vatican City, the smallest independent state in the world, located within the city of Rome, Italy. With an area of just 44 hectares (110 acres), Vatican City is home to the spiritual and administrative center of the Roman Catholic Church, including St. Peter's Basilica, the Vatican Museums, and the Sistine Chapel. Despite its diminutive size, Vatican City wields significant cultural and religious influence, attracting millions of visitors each year.

Another notable micro-nation is Monaco, a tiny principality nestled on the French Riviera. With an area of just 2.02 square kilometers (0.78 square miles), Monaco is the second-smallest country in the world after Vatican City. Despite its small size, Monaco is renowned for its opulent casinos, luxury hotels, and glamorous yacht-filled harbor. The principality also hosts the prestigious Monaco Grand Prix, one of the most iconic events in motorsports.

Moving to the Indian Ocean, we encounter the Maldives, an archipelago nation comprising 26 atolls and over 1,000 coral islands. With a total land area of just 298 square kilometers (115 square miles), the Maldives is the smallest Asian country in both land area and population. Despite its size, the Maldives is renowned for its stunning natural beauty, with pristine beaches, crystal-clear waters, and vibrant coral reefs attracting millions of tourists each year.

In Europe, Liechtenstein stands out as one of the smallest countries on the continent, nestled between Switzerland and Austria. With an area of just 160 square kilometers (62 square miles), Liechtenstein is a constitutional monarchy known for its picturesque Alpine landscapes, medieval castles, and low taxes. Despite its small size, Liechtenstein boasts one of the highest GDP per capita in the world, driven by its prosperous banking and financial services sector.

Beyond micro-nations, the world is also dotted with enclaves—territorial anomalies surrounded entirely by the territory of another country. One such example is San Marino, a landlocked micro-state enclaved within Italy. With an area of just 61 square kilometers (24 square miles), San Marino is one of the world's oldest republics and is known for its well-preserved medieval architecture and rich cultural heritage.

Bizarre Borders and Border Disputes

While borders are often seen as lines on a map, defining the limits of one country and the beginning of another, they can sometimes be anything but straightforward. Across the globe, there exist numerous examples of bizarre borders and ongoing disputes that reflect the complexities of geopolitics, history, and culture.

One of the most well-known examples of a bizarre border is the Baarle-Hertog/Baarle-Nassau enclave complex, located on the border between Belgium and the Netherlands. Within this small area, comprising several villages, the border between the two countries zigzags in a bewildering pattern, resulting in numerous enclaves and exclaves where one country's territory is entirely surrounded by the other. The situation is further complicated by the fact that some buildings and even rooms are divided by the border, leading to unique legal and administrative challenges for residents and authorities.

In South America, the tri-border area where Brazil, Argentina, and Paraguay meet is another example of complex borders and disputed territories. The convergence of the Iguazú and Paraná rivers creates a unique geopolitical situation, with each country vying for control over the strategic waterways and surrounding territories. The region is known for its bustling trade, smuggling, and illicit activities, fueled by the porous borders and jurisdictional ambiguities.

Similarly, the Kashmir region in South Asia has been the focal point of a protracted territorial dispute between India and Pakistan since the partition of British India in 1947. Both countries claim the region in its entirety, resulting in decades of conflict and several wars. The Line of Control, established after the Indo-Pakistani War of 1971, divides the region into Indian-administered territory and Pakistan-administered territory, with a small portion also controlled by China.

In Africa, the border between Botswana and Zambia along the Zambezi River is another example of a disputed territory with complex geopolitical implications. Known as the Kasikili/Sedudu Island dispute, the disagreement revolves around a small riverine island in the Zambezi River, which both countries claim as their own. The dispute has led to tensions between Botswana and Zambia and has been the subject of arbitration by international bodies.

Landlocked Countries and Their Challenges

Landlocked countries, those devoid of any coastline and entirely surrounded by other countries, face a unique set of challenges stemming from their geographical isolation. Despite their lack of access to the sea, these nations are often rich in cultural heritage, natural resources, and strategic significance. However, their landlocked status can present obstacles to economic development, transportation, and international trade.

One of the primary challenges faced by landlocked countries is the reliance on neighboring countries for access to seaports and international trade routes. Without direct access to the sea, landlocked nations must rely on their neighbors' infrastructure and transportation networks to import and export goods, which can result in higher transportation costs, delays, and logistical challenges. Additionally, landlocked countries may be more vulnerable to disruptions in trade routes or political instability in neighboring countries, which can impact their economies and access to essential goods and services.

Another challenge for landlocked countries is the development of efficient and cost-effective transportation infrastructure. Building and maintaining roads, railways, and other transportation networks to connect landlocked regions with international markets can be costly and technically challenging, particularly in rugged terrain or remote areas. Additionally, landlocked countries may face obstacles such as bureaucratic red tape, corruption, and political instability, which can hinder infrastructure development and economic growth.

Furthermore, landlocked countries may experience limited access to freshwater resources, as many rivers and lakes are shared with neighboring countries. Disputes over water rights and usage can arise, leading to tensions and conflicts between landlocked nations and their neighbors. Additionally, landlocked countries may face challenges related to land degradation, deforestation, and environmental degradation, which can impact agricultural productivity and food security.

Despite these challenges, many landlocked countries have managed to overcome their geographical limitations and achieve economic growth and development. Through strategic partnerships, investment in infrastructure, and diversification of their economies, landlocked nations can harness their unique strengths and capitalize on their natural resources to improve the livelihoods of their citizens and enhance their global competitiveness.

Island Nations: Independent Realms Surrounded by Water

Islands have long held a special fascination for humanity, offering isolated realms surrounded by the vastness of the ocean. Across the globe, there exist numerous island nations—sovereign states entirely encompassed by water—that boast unique cultures, histories, and identities. These independent realms, though small in size, wield significant influence and contribute to the rich tapestry of global diversity.

One such island nation is Japan, a fascinating archipelago comprising over 6,800 islands, of which the four main islands—Honshu, Hokkaido, Kyushu, and Shikoku—are home to the majority of the population.

Japan's insular geography has profoundly influenced its culture, shaping traditions, art, cuisine, and spirituality. From the tranquil temples of Kyoto to the bustling streets of Tokyo, Japan offers a captivating blend of ancient heritage and modern innovation, making it one of the most intriguing island nations in the world.

In the Indian Ocean, the island nation of Madagascar stands out as a biodiversity hotspot, renowned for its unique flora and fauna found nowhere else on Earth. As the fourth largest island in the world, Madagascar's isolation has led to the evolution of countless endemic species, including lemurs, chameleons, and baobab trees. Despite its ecological significance, Madagascar faces challenges related to deforestation, habitat loss, and environmental degradation, highlighting the delicate balance between human development and conservation efforts.

In the Caribbean Sea, the island nation of Jamaica captivates visitors with its vibrant culture, reggae music, and stunning natural beauty. From the lush rainforests of the Blue Mountains to the idyllic beaches of Negril and Montego Bay, Jamaica offers a wealth of attractions for travelers seeking sun, sand, and adventure. Despite its relatively small size, Jamaica has made significant contributions to global culture, from its iconic music and cuisine to its influential sports figures and literary talents.

Moving to the South Pacific, the island nation of Fiji is renowned for its pristine beaches, turquoise waters, and warm hospitality. Comprising over 300 islands, Fiji offers a diverse array of landscapes, from lush tropical rainforests and cascading waterfalls to vibrant coral reefs teeming with marine life. With its rich cultural heritage, including traditional Fijian ceremonies, dances, and rituals, Fiji offers visitors a glimpse into the enchanting world of Polynesian culture and hospitality.

Countries with Multiple Capitals

While most countries have a single capital city that serves as the seat of government and administrative center, there exist several unique nations with multiple capitals, each playing a distinct role in governance, culture, or history. These countries offer fascinating insights into the complexities of political organization, regional dynamics, and cultural diversity.

One notable example is South Africa, which has three designated capital cities: Pretoria (executive capital), Cape Town (legislative capital), and Bloemfontein (judicial capital). This arrangement, known as the "Tshwane Metropolis," reflects South Africa's diverse cultural and historical heritage, with each city representing different aspects of the country's identity. Pretoria, located in the Gauteng province, serves as the administrative capital, housing the executive branch of government and numerous government departments. Cape Town, situated in the Western Cape province, is home to the Parliament of South Africa and the legislative branch of government. Bloemfontein, located in the Free State province, hosts the country's highest court, the Supreme Court of Appeal, making it the judicial capital.

Similarly, Bolivia, located in South America, is another country with multiple capitals. The constitutional capital of Bolivia is Sucre, where the country's judicial branch is headquartered. However, La Paz serves as the de facto capital and the seat of government, housing the executive and legislative branches. La Paz's higher altitude and strategic location in the Andes mountains make it a vibrant cultural and economic center, while Sucre's colonial architecture and historic significance add to Bolivia's rich cultural heritage.

Another example is Malaysia, which has two capitals: Kuala Lumpur (legislative and executive capital) and Putrajaya (administrative capital). Kuala Lumpur, located in the state of Selangor, serves as Malaysia's economic and cultural hub, housing the Parliament of Malaysia, the Prime Minister's Office, and numerous government ministries. Putrajaya, on the other hand, was established in the 1990s as a planned city specifically designed to serve as the administrative center of the federal government. Putrajaya's modern infrastructure and iconic landmarks, such as the Putra Mosque and Putrajaya Convention Centre, reflect Malaysia's aspirations for administrative efficiency and urban development.

Chapter 4
Unusual Landforms and Landscapes

Surreal Deserts and Their Peculiarities

Deserts are among the most captivating and surreal landscapes on Earth, characterized by vast expanses of arid terrain, extreme temperatures, and unique geological formations. While deserts are often associated with barrenness and desolation, they are also home to a wealth of natural wonders and fascinating adaptations that defy expectations.

One of the most surreal deserts is the Namib Desert in southwestern Africa, renowned for its towering sand dunes, stark beauty, and otherworldly landscapes. Stretching along the Atlantic coast of Namibia, the Namib Desert is one of the oldest and driest deserts on Earth, with some areas receiving less than 2 millimeters of rainfall per year. Despite its harsh conditions, the Namib is teeming with life, from desert-adapted plants and insects to iconic species such as the desert-adapted elephant and the endemic Welwitschia plant, which can live for over 1,000 years.

In North America, the White Sands National Park in New Mexico offers another surreal desert experience, with its vast expanse of gypsum sand dunes shimmering like a sea of white waves against the backdrop of the Tularosa Basin. Unlike traditional quartz-based sand, the gypsum sand of White Sands is exceptionally fine and pure, giving it a unique texture and luminous appearance. The dunes are constantly shifting and evolving, creating an ever-changing landscape that captivates visitors year-round.

In the Middle East, the Rub' al Khali, or Empty Quarter, is one of the largest continuous sand deserts in the world, covering much of the Arabian Peninsula. Characterized by towering sand dunes, ancient fossil beds, and dramatic sandstone formations, the Rub' al Khali is one of the most inhospitable and least explored regions on Earth. Despite its harsh conditions, the desert is home to a rich cultural heritage and a wealth of biodiversity, including rare species such as the Arabian oryx and the sand cat.

One of the most surreal features of deserts is their ability to support life in seemingly inhospitable conditions. From cacti and succulents adapted to store water to nocturnal animals that emerge only after sunset to avoid the scorching heat, deserts are home to a remarkable array of flora and fauna that have evolved ingenious strategies for survival. Moreover, deserts are also repositories of geological treasures, with ancient rock formations, petrified forests, and fossilized remains offering glimpses into Earth's distant past.

Mesmerizing Caves and Underground Wonders

Beneath the surface of the Earth lie hidden worlds of breathtaking beauty and mystery, where stalactites drip like chandeliers and underground rivers carve intricate passages through ancient rock. From expansive limestone caverns to glittering crystal grottoes, caves offer a glimpse into the extraordinary geological forces that shape our planet and the timeless wonders that lie beneath.

One of the most mesmerizing caves in the world is the Son Doong Cave in Vietnam, the largest cave passage ever discovered. This colossal underground chamber stretches for over 5 kilometers in length and reaches heights of over 200 meters, creating a surreal subterranean landscape unlike anything else on Earth. Inside the Son Doong Cave, visitors encounter towering stalagmites, cascading waterfalls, and lush vegetation, illuminated by shafts of sunlight that penetrate the cave's massive ceiling openings.

Another awe-inspiring cave complex is the Caves of Aggtelek Karst and Slovak Karst, a Heritage Site spanning the border between Hungary and Slovakia. This network of over 700 caves features some of the most impressive stalactite and stalagmite formations in the world, including the breathtaking Baradla-Domica Cave, which stretches for over 25 kilometers and is adorned with intricate limestone formations and underground lakes.

In Mexico's Yucatán Peninsula, the Cenotes of the Riviera Maya offer a unique opportunity to explore underground rivers and sinkholes formed by the collapse of limestone bedrock. These crystal-clear pools of freshwater are revered by the ancient Maya civilization as sacred portals to the underworld, and today they attract visitors from around the world seeking to swim, snorkel, and dive in their pristine waters.

Moving to Europe, the Eisriesenwelt Ice Cave in Austria is a surreal wonderland of frozen beauty, with massive ice formations and frozen waterfalls that glitter like diamonds in the dim light. Spanning over 42 kilometers in length, Eisriesenwelt is the largest ice cave in the world, offering visitors a chance to explore its otherworldly chambers and marvel at the natural sculptures created by centuries of ice formation.

Beyond their sheer beauty, caves also play a vital role in scientific research and exploration, offering insights into Earth's geological history, climate change, and biodiversity. From ancient cave paintings and fossils to unique ecosystems and geological formations, caves are treasure troves of knowledge waiting to be discovered and explored.

Enigmatic Plateaus and High-Altitude Landscapes

High-altitude landscapes and plateaus present some of the most captivating and enigmatic features on Earth, characterized by their rugged terrain, dramatic vistas, and unique ecosystems. From the majestic plateaus of Tibet to the surreal beauty of the Altiplano in South America, these high-altitude regions offer a glimpse into the dynamic forces that shape our planet's surface and support diverse forms of life.

One of the most iconic high-altitude landscapes is the Tibetan Plateau, often referred to as the "Roof of the World." Situated in Central Asia, the Tibetan Plateau is the highest and largest plateau on Earth, covering an area of over 2.5 million square kilometers and averaging an elevation of over 4,500 meters above sea level. This vast expanse of high-altitude terrain is home to some of the world's highest peaks, including Mount Everest and the Himalayas, as well as vast grasslands, alpine meadows, and sacred lakes.

Despite its harsh conditions and extreme climate, the Tibetan Plateau supports a rich diversity of flora and fauna, including unique species adapted to the high-altitude environment. The plateau is also home to a vibrant culture and ancient traditions, with Tibetan Buddhism playing a central role in shaping the region's spiritual and cultural identity.

In South America, the Altiplano is another remarkable high-altitude landscape, stretching across the Andes Mountains and spanning parts of Bolivia, Peru, Chile, and Argentina. This vast plateau sits at an average elevation of over 3,750 meters above sea level, making it one of the highest inhabited regions in the world. The Altiplano is renowned for its stunning landscapes, including salt flats, volcanoes, and highland lakes such as Lake Titicaca, the largest lake in South America by volume.

The unique geography and climate of the Altiplano have given rise to a diverse array of ecosystems and cultural traditions, with indigenous communities such as the Aymara and Quechua peoples thriving amidst the harsh conditions. The region is also home to several archaeological sites and ancient ruins, including the famous Inca city of Machu Picchu, which sits atop a mountain ridge overlooking the Sacred Valley of the Incas.

In Africa, the Ethiopian Highlands offer another glimpse into the world of high-altitude landscapes, with rugged mountains, deep gorges, and fertile plateaus. This region is known for its rich biodiversity, including unique species such as the Ethiopian wolf and the gelada baboon, as well as its cultural heritage, with ancient rock-hewn churches and monasteries dotting the landscape.

Striking Rock Formations Around the Globe

From towering monoliths to intricate arches carved by the forces of wind and water, the world is dotted with breathtaking rock formations that captivate the imagination and inspire awe. These geological wonders, shaped over millions of years by erosion, tectonic activity, and other natural forces, offer a glimpse into the dynamic processes that have sculpted our planet's surface.

One of the most iconic rock formations is the towering sandstone pillars of Monument Valley, located on the border of Arizona and Utah in the United States. These majestic rock formations, known as buttes, mesas, and spires, rise hundreds of meters above the desert floor, creating a surreal landscape that has served as the backdrop for countless films, photographs, and works of art. Monument Valley is sacred to the Navajo Nation, who consider it a place of spiritual significance and cultural heritage.

Moving to Europe, the Giant's Causeway in Northern Ireland is a geological marvel composed of tens of thousands of hexagonal basalt columns formed by volcanic activity over 60 million years ago. Legend has it that the causeway was built as a pathway to Scotland, where he planned to challenge his Scottish rival.

In South America, the towering granite spires of Torres del Paine National Park in Chilean Patagonia offer a mesmerizing display of natural beauty. Carved by glaciers and sculpted by the elements, these jagged peaks rise dramatically from the windswept plains, creating a dramatic backdrop for hikers, climbers, and photographers. The park is also home to pristine lakes, ancient forests, and diverse wildlife, making it a paradise for nature lovers and outdoor enthusiasts.

The Marvels of Glaciers and Ice Formations

Glaciers and ice formations are among the most mesmerizing and awe-inspiring features of our planet's landscapes, sculpting the Earth's surface with their immense power and beauty. From towering ice caps to intricate ice caves, these frozen wonders offer a glimpse into the dynamic forces that shape our world and the delicate balance of climate and geology.

One of the most iconic glacier landscapes is found in the polar regions, where vast ice sheets cover much of the landmasses of Antarctica and Greenland. Antarctica, the coldest and driest continent on Earth, is home to the world's largest ice sheet, which contains about 70% of the Earth's fresh water. The Antarctic Ice Sheet is over 4.8 kilometers thick in some places and has been accumulating ice for millions of years, creating a pristine wilderness of icebergs, glaciers, and snow-capped mountains.

In the Northern Hemisphere, Greenland's ice sheet is the second-largest in the world and plays a critical role in regulating global sea levels and climate patterns. The Greenland Ice Sheet covers an area of over 1.7 million square kilometers and contains enough ice to raise global sea levels by over 7 meters if it were to melt entirely. Despite its remote location and harsh climate, Greenland's ice sheet supports a unique ecosystem of polar bears, Arctic foxes, and other cold-adapted species.

Beyond the polar regions, glaciers and ice formations can be found in mountainous regions around the world, from the Andes of South America to the Himalayas of Asia. One of the most famous glacier landscapes is the Perito Moreno Glacier in Argentina's Los Glaciares National Park. This massive glacier spans over 250 square kilometers and is renowned for its dynamic behavior, with frequent calving events that send towering icebergs crashing into the surrounding lake.

In Iceland, the Vatnajökull Glacier is Europe's largest ice cap, covering an area of over 8,100 square kilometers and reaching thicknesses of up to 1,000 meters. Beneath the glacier lies a world of ice caves, tunnels, and crevasses, created by the movement of meltwater and volcanic activity. These ice formations offer a surreal and otherworldly landscape that attracts photographers, adventurers, and nature lovers from around the world.

Chapter 5
Cultural Festivals and Celebrations

Carnivals: Vibrant Celebrations Around the World

Carnivals are vibrant and colorful celebrations that take place in many countries around the world, typically preceding the Lenten season and offering communities a chance to revel in music, dance, and spectacle. These lively events often feature elaborate parades, dazzling costumes, and spirited performances that showcase the unique cultural heritage and traditions of each region.

One of the most famous carnivals is the Rio Carnival in Brazil, renowned for its exuberance, energy, and sheer scale. Held in Rio de Janeiro each year before Lent, the Rio Carnival attracts millions of visitors from around the world who come to witness the dazzling parades, samba competitions, and street parties that take over the city's streets. The highlight of the Rio Carnival is the samba parade, where samba schools compete for the title of champion with elaborate floats, intricate costumes, and synchronized dance routines that reflect Brazil's rich cultural diversity.

In the Caribbean, the Trinidad and Tobago Carnival is another iconic celebration known for its vibrant costumes, pulsating music, and infectious energy. Held annually in the weeks leading up to Lent, the Trinidad and Tobago Carnival features calypso competitions, steelpan performances, and elaborate masquerade bands known as "mas." Participants spend months preparing their costumes, which often feature elaborate headdresses, sequins, and feathers, creating a kaleidoscope of color and creativity on the streets of Port of Spain.

In Europe, the Carnival of Venice in Italy is renowned for its elegant masks, elaborate costumes, and masquerade balls that harken back to the city's rich Renaissance heritage. Held in the weeks leading up to Lent, the Carnival of Venice attracts thousands of visitors who come to admire the intricate mask designs, attend extravagant parties, and participate in traditional events such as the Grand Canal parade and the Flight of the Angel.

In the Caribbean, the Junkanoo Festival in the Bahamas is a vibrant celebration of Afro-Bahamian culture and heritage, featuring colorful costumes, lively music, and energetic dance performances. Held annually on Boxing Day (December 26) and New Year's Day, the Junkanoo Festival pays homage to the island's African roots and traditions, with participants parading through the streets in elaborate costumes made from cardboard, crepe paper, and decorative elements.

Unique New Year's Traditions and Customs

New Year's Eve, the transition from one year to the next, is celebrated with enthusiasm and anticipation around the world. While the essence of the occasion remains the same—to bid farewell to the old year and welcome the new—different cultures have developed their own unique traditions and customs to mark the occasion. From ancient rituals to modern festivities, these diverse New Year's traditions offer a fascinating glimpse into the richness of global culture.

1. **Scotland's Hogmanay:** In Scotland, Hogmanay is celebrated with great gusto, often lasting several days and incorporating a mix of ancient customs and modern festivities. One of the most famous traditions is "First Footing," where the first person to enter a home after midnight brings gifts such as whiskey, shortbread, or coal to symbolize good luck and prosperity for the coming year. The streets of Edinburgh come alive with torchlight processions, fireworks, and music festivals, making it one of the world's largest New Year's celebrations.

2. **Spain's Grapes of Luck:** In Spain, it is customary to eat twelve grapes at the stroke of midnight on New Year's Eve, one for each chime of the clock. This tradition, known as the "12 grapes of luck," is believed to bring prosperity and good fortune for each month of the coming year. Spaniards gather in town squares to eat their grapes and watch the clock tower, with televised broadcasts showing the countdown from Madrid's Puerta del Sol.

3. **Japan's Joya no Kane:** In Japan, New Year's Eve is a time for reflection and renewal, with families gathering for a traditional meal called "osechi ryori" and visiting temples at midnight to hear the ringing of the temple bells, known as "joya no kane." The bells are rung 108 times, representing the 108 human sins in Buddhist belief, and are said to cleanse the soul and bring good luck for the new year.

4. Ecuador's Burning Effigies: In Ecuador, the New Year is celebrated with the tradition of burning effigies, or "año viejos," which represent the old year. These effigies, often made from paper or straw, are filled with firecrackers and set ablaze at midnight to symbolize the burning away of past troubles and negativity, making way for a fresh start in the new year.

5. Denmark's Plate Smashing: In Denmark, it is a tradition to save old dishes and plates throughout the year and then throw them at the doors of friends and family on New Year's Eve. This custom, known as "smashing plates," is believed to bring good luck and symbolize friendship and renewal. In some parts of Denmark, it is also common to leap off chairs at midnight to "jump" into the new year.

Intriguing Religious Festivals and Ceremonies

Religious festivals and ceremonies are an integral part of cultural heritage around the world, offering communities an opportunity to celebrate their faith, express gratitude, and strengthen social bonds. These festivals often blend ancient traditions with modern customs, creating vibrant and colorful celebrations that reflect the spiritual beliefs and values of each culture. Here are some examples of intriguing religious festivals and ceremonies from different parts of the world:

1. Diwali (India):
   Diwali, also known as the Festival of Lights, is one of the most significant Hindu festivals celebrated across India and by Hindu communities worldwide. The festival symbolizes the victory of light over darkness and good over evil, and it typically lasts for five days. During Diwali, homes and streets are adorned with oil lamps, candles, and colorful decorations, while families gather to pray, exchange gifts, and feast on traditional sweets. Fireworks displays and cultural performances are also common during Diwali celebrations.

2. Holi (India):

Holi, also known as the Festival of Colors, is a vibrant Hindu festival celebrated primarily in India and Nepal. The festival marks the arrival of spring and the triumph of good over evil, and it is celebrated with great enthusiasm and joy. During Holi, people gather in public spaces to engage in playful activities, such as throwing colored powders and water at each other, singing and dancing, and enjoying festive foods and drinks. Holi is also a time for reconciliation and forgiveness, as people come together to bury past grievances and start anew.

3. Semana Santa (Spain):

Semana Santa, or Holy Week, is a significant religious observance in Spain and other predominantly Catholic countries. The week leading up to Easter Sunday is marked by solemn processions, elaborate floats depicting scenes from the Passion of Christ, and religious rituals. Each day of Semana Santa has its own set of customs and traditions, with cities like Seville and Malaga hosting some of the most elaborate and dramatic processions in the country. Semana Santa is a time for reflection, prayer, and spiritual renewal for Catholics around the world.

4. Songkran (Thailand):

Songkran is the Thai New Year festival, celebrated annually in April with water fights, street parties, and religious ceremonies. The festival marks the end of the dry season and the beginning of the traditional Thai New Year, and it is observed with rituals such as visiting temples, making offerings to monks, and pouring water over Buddha statues as a symbol of cleansing and purification. Songkran is also famous for its lively water fights, where people of all ages douse each other with water as a playful way to welcome the new year and cool off from the heat.

5. Day of the Dead (Mexico):

Dia de los Muertos, or Day of the Dead, is a Mexican holiday that honors deceased loved ones and celebrates the continuity of life and death. The holiday, which takes place on November 1st and 2nd, coincides with the Catholic observances of All Saints' Day and All Souls' Day. Families create colorful altars, or ofrendas, adorned with photographs, candles, flowers, and favorite foods of the deceased, to welcome their spirits back to the world of the living. Day of the Dead is a time for remembrance, reflection, and celebration of the enduring bonds between the living and the dead.

Harvest Festivals: Celebrating Nature's Bounty

Harvest festivals are joyous celebrations held around the world to mark the end of the agricultural season and give thanks for the bounty of the harvest. These festivals are deeply rooted in agricultural traditions and cultural heritage, bringing communities together to celebrate abundance, share food, and express gratitude to the land and the gods for their blessings. From ancient rituals to modern festivities, harvest festivals offer a colorful and vibrant celebration of nature's abundance and the cycle of life.

1. Thanksgiving (United States):

Thanksgiving is one of the most widely celebrated harvest festivals in the world, observed annually on the fourth Thursday of November in the United States. The holiday traces its origins to a 1621 feast shared by the Pilgrims and Native Americans in Plymouth, Massachusetts, to give thanks for a successful harvest. Today, Thanksgiving is celebrated with family gatherings, feasts featuring traditional dishes such as roasted turkey, pumpkin pie, and cranberry sauce, and expressions of gratitude for blessings and abundance.

2. Chuseok (South Korea):

Chuseok, also known as the Korean Thanksgiving, is a major harvest festival celebrated in South Korea and by Korean communities around the world. The festival typically takes place in September or October and lasts for three days, during which families gather to honor their ancestors, visit ancestral graves, and share food and gifts. Traditional Chuseok foods include songpyeon (rice cakes filled with sweet fillings), freshly harvested fruits, and other seasonal delicacies.

3. Pongal (India):

Pongal is a Tamil harvest festival celebrated primarily in the Indian state of Tamil Nadu and in other parts of South India. The festival, which typically takes place in January, coincides with the winter solstice and marks the beginning of the sun's northward journey, known as Uttarayanam. Pongal is celebrated with the preparation of a special dish called "pongal," made from newly harvested rice, lentils, jaggery, and spices. The festival also includes rituals such as boiling milk until it overflows, signifying abundance and prosperity.

4. Mid-Autumn Festival (China):

The Mid-Autumn Festival, also known as the Mooncake Festival, is a harvest festival celebrated by Chinese communities around the world. The festival takes place on the 15th day of the eighth month of the lunar calendar, when the moon is at its fullest and brightest. Families gather to admire the full moon, eat mooncakes (sweet pastries filled with lotus seed paste or other fillings), and share meals together. Lanterns are also lit and carried in parades to symbolize the brightness of the harvest moon.

5. Lammas (Europe):

Lammas, also known as Lughnasadh, is an ancient Celtic festival celebrated in parts of Europe, particularly in Ireland, Scotland, and England. The festival marks the beginning of the harvest season and is named after the Celtic god Lugh, who was associated with agriculture and light. Lammas is celebrated with feasting, dancing, and rituals honoring the land and the spirits of nature. Traditionally, a loaf of bread made from the first harvested grain is baked and offered as a symbol of thanks and abundance.

Quirky and Offbeat Festivals That Capture Attention

While many festivals around the world celebrate traditional themes such as harvest, religion, or cultural heritage, there are also a plethora of quirky and offbeat festivals that showcase the unique creativity and eccentricity of human culture. From bizarre competitions to wacky traditions, these festivals offer a delightful glimpse into the playful and imaginative side of humanity. Here are some examples of quirky and offbeat festivals that capture attention:

1. La Tomatina (Spain):

La Tomatina is an annual festival held in the town of Buñol, Spain, where participants engage in a massive tomato fight. Thousands of people gather in the streets to pelt each other with ripe tomatoes, creating a messy and colorful spectacle that attracts visitors from around the world. La Tomatina takes place on the last Wednesday of August and is accompanied by music, dancing, and festivities.

2. Cheese Rolling Festival (United Kingdom):

The Cheese Rolling Festival is a quirky event held annually on the Spring Bank Holiday at Cooper's Hill in Gloucestershire, England. During the festival, a large wheel of cheese is rolled down a steep hill, and participants race after it in pursuit. The first person to reach the bottom of the hill and grab the cheese is declared the winner. The event has become so popular that people from around the world come to compete or simply watch the spectacle unfold.

3. Boryeong Mud Festival (South Korea):

The Boryeong Mud Festival is an annual event held in Boryeong, South Korea, where participants engage in various mud-related activities and competitions. The festival was originally created to promote the health benefits of the local mud, which is rich in minerals and believed to have therapeutic properties. Activities at the festival include mud wrestling, mudslides, and mud baths, as well as live music, food stalls, and cultural performances.

4. Wife Carrying World Championships (Finland):

The Wife Carrying World Championships is a quirky competition held annually in Sonkajärvi, Finland, where male contestants race through an obstacle course while carrying their female partners on their backs. The origins of the competition are unclear, but it is believed to have originated from an ancient Finnish tradition known as "pillage and plunder." Today, the event attracts competitors from around the world who compete for the title of World Champion and the prize of the wife's weight in beer.

5. Frozen Dead Guy Days (United States):

Frozen Dead Guy Days is an annual festival held in Nederland, Colorado, that celebrates the bizarre story of Grandpa Bredo Morstoel, whose frozen corpse is stored in a cryonic chamber in the town. The festival features a variety of quirky events and activities, including coffin races, polar plunges, frozen turkey bowling, and live music performances. Frozen Dead Guy Days attracts thousands of visitors each year and has become a beloved tradition in the quirky mountain town.

Chapter 6
Language Wonders

The Most Spoken Languages in the World

Language is a cornerstone of human communication and culture, with thousands of languages spoken across the globe. However, a few languages stand out as the most widely spoken, serving as crucial tools for international communication, trade, and cultural exchange. Here are the most spoken languages in the world based on the number of native speakers:

1. Mandarin Chinese:

With over 1 billion native speakers, Mandarin Chinese is the most spoken language in the world. It is the official language of China and Taiwan and is also widely spoken in Singapore and among Chinese diaspora communities worldwide. Mandarin Chinese is part of the Sino-Tibetan language family and is characterized by its tonal nature, with four main tones that change the meaning of words.

2. Spanish:

Spanish is the second most spoken language in the world, with approximately 460 million native speakers. It is the official language of 21 countries, including Spain, Mexico, Colombia, Argentina, and many others in Latin America. Spanish is also one of the six official languages of the United Nations and is widely spoken in the United States, where it is the second most spoken language after English.

3. English:

English is the third most spoken language in the world, with around 360 million native speakers. However, when including non-native speakers, English becomes the most widely spoken language globally. English is the official language of 67 countries and is used as a lingua franca in many parts of the world for international communication, business, science, and technology.

4. Hindi:

Hindi is the fourth most spoken language in the world, with approximately 341 million native speakers. It is the official language of India and is spoken widely across the Indian subcontinent. Hindi is part of the Indo-Aryan language family and shares many similarities with Urdu, the official language of Pakistan.

5. Bengali:

Bengali, also known as Bangla, is the fifth most spoken language in the world, with around 228 million native speakers. It is the official language of Bangladesh and the Indian state of West Bengal, as well as being spoken in parts of the Indian states of Assam and Tripura. Bengali is known for its rich literary tradition, with works by poets such as Rabindranath Tagore earning international acclaim.

Languages with Unique Alphabets and Scripts

Human language is expressed through a diverse array of alphabets and writing systems, each with its own unique symbols and characters. While some languages use familiar alphabets like the Latin script used in English, others have developed intricate and fascinating writing systems that reflect their rich cultural heritage and linguistic complexity. Here are some languages with unique alphabets and scripts:

1. Ge'ez Script (Ethiopic):

The Ge'ez script is an ancient writing system used for the Ethiopian Semitic languages, including Amharic and Tigrinya. It originated in the ancient kingdom of Aksum (present-day Ethiopia and Eritrea) and is one of the oldest alphabets still in use today. The Ge'ez script is notable for its distinctive characters, which are based on ancient South Arabian scripts and are written from left to right.

2. Hangul (Korean):

Hangul is the native alphabet of the Korean language and was created in the 15th century by King Sejong the Great of Korea. Unlike many writing systems, Hangul is phonetic and was specifically designed to be easy to learn and use. Hangul characters are composed of simple geometric shapes, which represent the phonetic sounds of the language. The creation of Hangul is considered a significant achievement in linguistic history and is celebrated in South Korea with Hangul Day on October 9th.

3. Inuktitut Syllabics (Inuit):

Inuktitut Syllabics is a writing system used for the Inuit languages of Canada, including Inuktitut and Inuinnaqtun. Developed in the 19th century by Christian missionaries, Inuktitut Syllabics is based on the Cree syllabary and is used to write the indigenous languages of the Canadian Arctic. The script consists of symbols representing syllables rather than individual sounds, making it well-suited for representing the complex phonetics of the Inuit languages.

4. Arabic Script (Arabic):

The Arabic script is one of the most widely used writing systems in the world and is used for writing the Arabic language as well as several other languages, including Persian, Urdu, and Pashto. It is an abjad script, meaning that it primarily represents consonants and relies on diacritical marks to indicate vowel sounds. The Arabic script is known for its elegant and flowing calligraphic styles and has a rich artistic tradition associated with it.

5. Ogham (Old Irish):

Ogham is an ancient alphabet used to write the Old Irish language and other Celtic languages of Ireland and Scotland. It consists of a series of strokes or notches carved into stone or wood, typically along the edge of a standing stone or monument. Ogham is read from bottom to top and was primarily used for short inscriptions and personal names. It is one of the earliest known forms of writing in Ireland and provides valuable insights into the early history and culture of the Celtic peoples.

Endangered Languages and Language Preservation Efforts

Languages are not just means of communication; they are repositories of cultural heritage, identity, and knowledge. Unfortunately, many languages around the world are endangered, facing the threat of extinction due to factors such as globalization, urbanization, and government policies. Language preservation efforts aim to document, revitalize, and protect endangered languages, recognizing their importance in maintaining linguistic diversity and cultural richness.

Here's an overview of endangered languages and the initiatives aimed at their preservation:

1. Endangered Languages:

- It is estimated that there are over 7,000 languages spoken around the world, but a significant portion of them are endangered.
- The World's Languages in Danger identifies as vulnerable, endangered, or extinct based on factors such as the number of speakers, intergenerational transmission, and language vitality.
- Many indigenous and minority languages are particularly at risk, as they often face marginalization, discrimination, and pressure to assimilate into dominant languages and cultures.

2. Language Preservation Efforts:

- Documentation: Linguists and researchers work to document endangered languages through fieldwork, recordings, and written materials. This helps preserve linguistic data and provides a resource for future language revitalization efforts.
- Education: Language revitalization efforts often involve educational initiatives aimed at teaching endangered languages to younger generations. This can include language immersion programs, schools, and community-based language classes.
- Technology: Digital tools and resources, such as language learning apps, online dictionaries, and multimedia materials, are increasingly being used to support language preservation efforts and make endangered languages more accessible.
- Community Engagement: Language preservation is most effective when it involves active participation from the language-speaking community. Community-led initiatives, such as language revitalization workshops, cultural events, and storytelling sessions, help foster pride and interest in endangered languages.
- Policy and Advocacy: Governments, NGOs, and international organizations play a crucial role in supporting language preservation efforts through policies, funding, and advocacy. This includes recognizing the rights of linguistic minorities, promoting multilingual education, and supporting language documentation and revitalization projects.

3. Success Stories:

- There are numerous examples of successful language revitalization efforts around the world. For instance, the revitalization of the Maori language in New Zealand has been supported by government policies, educational initiatives, and community engagement, leading to increased numbers of speakers and a resurgence of Maori language and culture.

- Similarly, the revival of the Hebrew language in Israel is considered a remarkable success story of language revitalization. Despite being considered a dead language for centuries, Hebrew was revived as a spoken language in the late 19th and early 20th centuries through language planning efforts, educational reforms, and cultural revival movements.

Multilingual Countries and Communities

The world is home to a remarkable diversity of languages, with many countries and communities embracing multilingualism as a fundamental aspect of their cultural identity and social fabric. Multilingualism fosters communication, cultural exchange, and inclusivity, enriching societies and promoting understanding among people of different linguistic backgrounds. Here are some examples of multilingual countries and communities that showcase the richness of linguistic diversity:

1. Switzerland:

Switzerland is a prime example of a multilingual country, with four official languages: German, French, Italian, and Romansh. Each language is spoken in specific regions of the country, reflecting Switzerland's diverse linguistic and cultural heritage. German is the most widely spoken language, followed by French, Italian, and Romansh. Multilingualism is an integral part of Swiss identity, with many Swiss citizens proficient in multiple languages and code-switching between languages being common in daily life.

2. India:

India is another multilingual country with incredible linguistic diversity, boasting over 1,600 languages and dialects spoken across its vast territory. The Constitution of India recognizes 22 official languages, including Hindi, Bengali, Tamil, Telugu, Urdu, and Gujarati, among others. Multilingualism is deeply ingrained in Indian society, with many Indians proficient in multiple languages due to the country's diverse regional, linguistic, and cultural landscapes.

3. Canada:

Canada is a bilingual country with two official languages: English and French. English is the most widely spoken language, particularly in provinces like Ontario and British Columbia, while French is predominant in Quebec and parts of New Brunswick. Canada's bilingualism is enshrined in the Canadian Charter of Rights and Freedoms, and federal government services are provided in both English and French. Additionally, Canada is home to numerous Indigenous languages spoken by First Nations, Métis, and Inuit peoples, further adding to its linguistic diversity.

4. Belgium:

Belgium is a multilingual country with three official languages: Dutch, French, and German. Dutch is the majority language spoken by the Flemish population in the northern region of Flanders, while French is predominant in the southern region of Wallonia. German is spoken by a small minority in the eastern region of Wallonia. Belgium's linguistic diversity is reflected in its decentralized political structure, with regions and language communities having their own governments and language policies.

5. South Africa:

South Africa is a multilingual country with 11 official languages, reflecting its diverse population and cultural heritage. The official languages include isiZulu, isiXhosa, Afrikaans, English, Sepedi, Setswana, Sesotho, Xitsonga, siSwati, Tshivenda, and isiNdebele. Multilingualism is a cornerstone of South African society, with many South Africans proficient in multiple languages and code-switching between languages being common in everyday communication.

The Art of Whistled Languages and Unusual Communication

Human beings have developed ingenious ways to communicate across vast distances and challenging environments, often relying on non-traditional methods such as whistling, drumming, or even hand signals. One fascinating example of this is the art of whistled languages, where people communicate by whistling instead of speaking. Here, we explore the remarkable phenomenon of whistled languages and other unusual forms of communication:

1. Whistled Languages:

Whistled languages are unique forms of communication where words and sentences are expressed through whistling instead of spoken words. These languages are typically found in mountainous or forested regions where conventional spoken language may be difficult to hear over long distances. One of the most well-known examples of a whistled language is Silbo Gomero, used by inhabitants of La Gomera, a small island in the Canary Islands, Spain. Silbo Gomero consists of a series of whistled tones and pitch variations that correspond to different phonemes and syllables in the Spanish language. It was traditionally used by shepherds to communicate across the island's rugged terrain and is now taught in schools as part of the cultural heritage of La Gomera.

2. Drum Languages:

Drum languages, also known as drum telegraphy or talking drums, are communication systems where messages are conveyed through the rhythmic patterns of drums. These languages are found in various cultures across Africa and Asia, where drums are used to transmit messages over long distances. Each drumbeat corresponds to a specific word or phrase, and skilled drummers can convey complex messages by varying the tempo, pitch, and rhythm of their drumming. Drum languages have been used for purposes such as relaying news, coordinating hunts, and sending warnings of approaching danger.

3. Sign Languages:

Sign languages are visual-gestural communication systems used by deaf and hard-of-hearing individuals to communicate with each other and with hearing people. Unlike spoken languages, sign languages rely on hand gestures, facial expressions, and body movements to convey meaning. Sign languages are fully-fledged languages with their own grammatical rules and syntax, and they vary widely across different countries and regions. One of the most widely used sign languages is American Sign Language (ASL), which is used by deaf communities in the United States and parts of Canada.

4. Smoke Signals:

Smoke signals are a form of visual communication where messages are conveyed through the use of smoke signals. This method of communication has been used by indigenous peoples in various parts of the world, including North America, Africa, and Australia. By creating patterns of smoke with fires, people could convey messages across long distances, with different patterns representing different meanings. Smoke signals were often used for purposes such as signaling the presence of enemies, communicating between distant camps or villages, or sending messages during hunts or ceremonies.

Chapter 7
Historic Landmarks and Heritage Sites

Iconic Landmarks: From the Pyramids to the Taj Mahal

Throughout history, mankind has built remarkable structures that continue to awe and inspire people around the world. From ancient wonders to architectural marvels, these iconic landmarks stand as testaments to human ingenuity, creativity, and perseverance. Here are some of the world's most iconic landmarks, from the majestic Pyramids of Giza to the breathtaking Taj Mahal:

1. Pyramids of Giza (Egypt):

The Pyramids of Giza are perhaps the most famous ancient monuments in the world, located on the outskirts of Cairo, Egypt. Built over 4,500 years ago as royal tombs for pharaohs, the Great Pyramid of Giza is the largest and most famous of the three pyramids, standing at a height of 146 meters (481 feet). The precision engineering and massive scale of the pyramids continue to intrigue historians, archaeologists, and visitors alike, drawing millions of tourists to Egypt each year.

2. Taj Mahal (India):

The Taj Mahal is an iconic symbol of love and architectural beauty, located in Agra, India. Built in the 17th century by the Mughal emperor as a mausoleum for his beloved wife Mumtaz Mahal, the Taj Mahal is renowned for its stunning white marble dome, intricate carvings, and symmetrical gardens. Recognized as one of the New Seven Wonders of the World, the it attracts millions of visitors annually.

3. Eiffel Tower (France):

The Eiffel Tower is an iconic symbol of Paris and one of the most recognizable landmarks in the world. Designed by Gustave Eiffel and completed in 1889 for the Exposition Universelle (World's Fair), the wrought iron tower stands at a height of 324 meters (1,063 feet). Initially criticized by some as an eyesore, the Eiffel Tower has since become a beloved symbol of French culture and engineering prowess, attracting millions of visitors to its observation decks and restaurants each year.

4. Great Wall of China (China):

The Great Wall of China is an awe-inspiring feat of ancient engineering and one of the most iconic landmarks in the world. Stretching over 21,000 kilometers (13,000 miles) across northern China, the Great Wall was built over several centuries to protect China from invasions by nomadic tribes. Parts of the wall date back as far as the 7th century BCE, with the most famous sections built during the Ming Dynasty (1368-1644). Today, the Great Wall is a symbol of China's rich cultural heritage.

5. Statue of Liberty (United States):

The Statue of Liberty is a symbol of freedom and democracy, located on Liberty Island in New York Harbor, United States. Designed by French sculptor Frédéric Auguste Bartholdi and dedicated in 1886, the statue depicts a robed female figure representing Libertas, the Roman goddess of freedom, holding a torch and a tablet inscribed with the date of the American Declaration of Independence. A gift from France to the United States, the Statue of Liberty has welcomed millions of immigrants to America and remains an enduring symbol of hope and opportunity.

Ancient Ruins and Archaeological Marvels

Across the globe, ancient ruins and archaeological sites stand as silent witnesses to the rich tapestry of human history and civilization. These remnants of the past offer invaluable insights into the lives, cultures, and achievements of our ancestors, captivating the imagination and sparking curiosity about the mysteries of antiquity. Here are some remarkable ancient ruins and archaeological marvels that continue to fascinate and inspire people around the world:

1. Machu Picchu (Peru):

Machu Picchu is one of the most iconic archaeological sites in the world, nestled high in the Andes Mountains of Peru. Built by the Inca civilization in the 15th century, Machu Picchu is renowned for its stunning mountain setting, intricate stone terraces, and sophisticated engineering feats. This ancient citadel served as a royal estate and religious sanctuary, but its precise purpose remains a subject of debate among historians and archaeologists. Machu Picchu attracts millions of visitors each year.

2. Petra (Jordan):

Petra is an ancient city carved into the rose-red cliffs of southern Jordan, dating back to the 4th century BCE. Once a thriving trading hub and capital of the Nabatean Kingdom, Petra is famous for its monumental rock-cut architecture, including the iconic Treasury (Al-Khazneh) and the Monastery (Ad Deir). Accessible only through a narrow gorge known as the Siq, Petra's grandeur and beauty have earned it the nickname "Rose City." Petra is considered one of the New Seven Wonders of the World.

3. The Acropolis of Athens (Greece):

The Acropolis of Athens is a symbol of classical Greek civilization and the birthplace of democracy, located on a rocky outcrop overlooking the city of Athens. Dominated by the iconic Parthenon temple, the Acropolis is home to a collection of ancient ruins, including the Erechtheion, the Propylaea, and the Temple of Athena Nike. These architectural masterpieces date back to the 5th century BCE and are renowned for their harmonious proportions, refined craftsmanship, and enduring cultural significance.

4. The Great Sphinx and Pyramids of Giza (Egypt):

The Great Sphinx and Pyramids of Giza are among the most recognizable symbols of ancient Egypt, located on the outskirts of Cairo. Built over 4,500 years ago during the Old Kingdom period, the Great Sphinx is a colossal limestone statue depicting a mythical creature with the body of a lion and the head of a human. Nearby, the Pyramids of Giza, including the Great Pyramid of Khufu, the Pyramid of Khafre, and the Pyramid of Menkaure, are monumental tombs constructed for pharaohs. These ancient structures are marvels of engineering and continue to captivate visitors with their enigmatic beauty and historical significance.

5. Angkor Wat (Cambodia):

Angkor Wat is a sprawling temple complex and the largest religious monument in the world, located in Cambodia's Siem Reap province. Built in the early 12th century by the Khmer Empire, Angkor Wat is a masterpiece of Khmer architecture, featuring intricate bas-reliefs, towering spires, and vast courtyards. Originally dedicated to the Hindu god Vishnu and later transformed into a Buddhist temple, Angkor Wat symbolizes the spiritual and cultural heritage of Cambodia. Angkor Wat is a symbol of national pride and identity for the Cambodian people.

Hidden Gems: Lesser-Known Heritage Sites

While iconic landmarks such as the Pyramids of Giza or the Taj Mahal capture global attention, there are countless lesser-known heritage sites scattered across the world that are equally deserving of recognition and appreciation. These hidden gems may lack the fame of their more celebrated counterparts, but they possess a unique charm, historical significance, and cultural richness that make them worthy destinations for intrepid travelers and history enthusiasts. Here are some remarkable lesser-known heritage sites from around the globe:

1. Hattusa (Turkey):
   Hattusa, located in modern-day Turkey, was the capital of the Hittite Empire during the late Bronze Age. This ancient city flourished between the 17th and 12th centuries BCE and was an important center of politics, religion, and commerce in the ancient Near East. Today, Hattusa is a Heritage Site known for its well-preserved ruins, including massive stone walls, royal palaces, temples, and gateways adorned with intricate reliefs.

2. Rapa Nui National Park (Easter Island, Chile):
   Rapa Nui National Park, located on Easter Island in the Pacific Ocean, is home to one of the world's most enigmatic archaeological sites: the moai statues. Carved by the indigenous Rapa Nui people between the 13th and 16th centuries, these colossal stone figures dot the island's landscape, standing as silent guardians over the land. In addition to the moai, Rapa Nui National Park features ancient petroglyphs, ceremonial platforms (ahu), and unique natural landscapes, making it a captivating destination for visitors interested in Polynesian history and culture.

3. Baalbek (Lebanon):

Baalbek is an ancient city located in the Beqaa Valley of Lebanon, known for its impressive Roman ruins and colossal stone temples. The most famous structure at Baalbek is the Temple of Bacchus, one of the best-preserved Roman temples in the world, dedicated to the god of wine and revelry. Nearby, the Temple of Jupiter and the Temple of Venus showcase the grandeur and architectural mastery of the Roman Empire. Baalbek is a testament to Lebanon's rich cultural heritage and historical significance.

4. Rock-Hewn Churches of Lalibela (Ethiopia):

The Rock-Hewn Churches of Lalibela, located in the highlands of northern Ethiopia, are a remarkable collection of monolithic churches carved from solid rock. Built in the 12th and 13th centuries, these awe-inspiring structures are considered one of the world's greatest architectural achievements and a center of pilgrimage for Ethiopian Orthodox Christians. Lalibela's churches are intricately carved and connected by a network of tunnels and passages, creating a mystical and spiritual atmosphere that draws visitors from around the world.

5. Göreme National Park and the Rock Sites of Cappadocia (Turkey):

Göreme National Park and the Rock Sites of Cappadocia, located in central Turkey, are renowned for their surreal landscapes, fairy chimneys, and rock-cut settlements. Dating back to the Byzantine period, these ancient cave dwellings and churches were carved into the soft volcanic tuff by early Christian communities seeking refuge from persecution. The underground cities of Derinkuyu and Kaymaklı are also highlights of the region, showcasing the ingenuity and resilience of ancient civilizations.

Chapter 8
Culinary Delights Around the World

Exotic Street Foods and Culinary Adventures

One of the most exciting ways to explore a new culture is through its street food. From bustling markets to roadside stalls, street food offers a tantalizing array of flavors, aromas, and textures that reflect the unique culinary traditions of a region. Embarking on a culinary adventure through exotic street foods allows travelers to immerse themselves in the vibrant tapestry of global gastronomy and experience the thrill of discovering new and unexpected flavors. Here are some mouthwatering examples of exotic street foods and culinary delights from around the world:

1. Banh Mi (Vietnam):

Banh Mi is a popular Vietnamese street food that combines French and Vietnamese culinary influences. This delectable sandwich features a crispy baguette filled with a variety of savory ingredients such as grilled pork, pâté, pickled vegetables, cilantro, and chili peppers. Bursting with contrasting flavors and textures, Banh Mi is a beloved street food enjoyed by locals and visitors alike in bustling markets and food stalls across Vietnam.

2. Takoyaki (Japan):

Takoyaki is a beloved Japanese street food that originated in Osaka and has since become a nationwide favorite. These bite-sized savory snacks are made from a batter of wheat flour, eggs, and dashi broth, filled with diced octopus, pickled ginger, and green onions, and cooked in a special takoyaki pan until golden brown and crispy on the outside. Takoyaki is typically served hot and topped with savory sauces, mayonnaise, bonito flakes, and dried seaweed.

3. Arepa (Colombia and Venezuela):

Arepa is a traditional South American street food that is popular in Colombia and Venezuela. These versatile cornmeal patties can be grilled, baked, or fried and are typically filled with a variety of savory ingredients such as cheese, shredded meat, avocado, beans, or eggs. Arepas are a staple of street food culture in both countries and are enjoyed as a quick and satisfying snack or meal any time of day.

4. Pani Puri (India):

Pani Puri, also known as Golgappa or Phuchka, is a beloved street food snack found throughout India. This crispy, hollow puri is filled with a spicy and tangy mixture of flavored water, tamarind chutney, chickpeas, potatoes, and spices. Pani Puri is typically served in small, bite-sized portions and is enjoyed for its refreshing flavors and playful presentation. It's a must-try street food for adventurous foodies exploring the vibrant culinary scene of India.

5. Börek (Turkey):

Börek is a savory pastry that is a staple of Turkish cuisine and a popular street food snack in Turkey and neighboring countries. This flaky pastry is typically filled with a variety of ingredients such as cheese, spinach, minced meat, or potatoes, seasoned with herbs and spices, and baked until golden brown and crispy. Börek is enjoyed as a quick and satisfying snack or appetizer and is often sold in bakeries, street stalls, and markets throughout Turkey.

6. Churros (Spain):

Churros are a classic Spanish street food favorite, consisting of fried dough pastry that is crispy on the outside and soft and fluffy on the inside. These golden-brown delights are typically dusted with sugar and cinnamon and served with a cup of thick chocolate dipping sauce for a decadent and indulgent treat. Churros are a beloved snack enjoyed by locals and visitors alike in bustling markets, plazas, and street corners throughout Spain.

Unique Local Delicacies and Regional Specialties

One of the joys of traveling is indulging in the diverse array of unique local delicacies and regional specialties that each destination has to offer. From exotic fruits and spices to traditional dishes passed down through generations, these culinary treasures reflect the rich cultural heritage and gastronomic traditions of a particular region. Here are some examples of unique local delicacies and regional specialties from around the world that are sure to tantalize the taste buds:

1. Balut (Philippines):

Balut is a popular street food delicacy in the Philippines that consists of a fertilized duck embryo that is boiled and eaten from the shell. Considered a delicacy and aphrodisiac, balut is typically seasoned with salt, vinegar, and chili peppers and enjoyed as a savory snack or appetizer.

2. Poutine (Canada):

Poutine is a quintessential Canadian dish that originated in the province of Quebec. This indulgent comfort food features crispy French fries smothered in rich gravy and topped with cheese curds. Poutine variations may include additional toppings such as pulled pork, bacon, or caramelized onions.

3. Haggis (Scotland):

Haggis is a traditional Scottish dish made from sheep's heart, liver, and lungs, mixed with oats, onions, and spices, and cooked in a sheep's stomach. Despite its unusual ingredients and preparation method, haggis is considered a delicacy in Scotland and is often served with neeps (turnips) and tatties (potatoes) on Burns Night, a celebration of the Scottish poet Robert Burns.

4. Surströmming (Sweden):

Surströmming is a pungent fermented fish delicacy that is native to Sweden. This traditional dish features Baltic herring that has been fermented in brine for several months, resulting in a strong, acidic odor. Surströmming is typically enjoyed on crispbread with butter, onions, and potatoes, and is often accompanied by schnapps to help mask the intense flavor.

5. Mofongo (Puerto Rico):

Mofongo is a popular Puerto Rican dish made from fried green plantains that are mashed with garlic, olive oil, and pork cracklings (chicharrones). The mixture is then shaped into balls or patties and served with a savory sauce or stew. Mofongo is a beloved comfort food in Puerto Rico and can be found in many traditional restaurants and eateries throughout the island.

6. Kangaroo Meat (Australia):

Kangaroo meat is a unique and sustainable protein source that is enjoyed by Indigenous Australians and has gained popularity in modern Australian cuisine. Kangaroo meat is lean, flavorful, and low in fat, making it a healthy alternative to traditional meats such as beef or lamb. It is often prepared as steaks, burgers, or sausages and is served with a variety of accompaniments such as roasted vegetables or native herbs.

The Art of Tea and Coffee: Cultural Brews

Tea and coffee are more than just beverages; they are cultural staples that have shaped societies, traditions, and rituals around the world for centuries. From elaborate tea ceremonies in Asia to bustling coffeehouses in Europe, the art of brewing and enjoying tea and coffee reflects the unique cultural heritage and social customs of different regions. Here's a look at some of the fascinating cultural brews associated with tea and coffee:

Tea:

1. **Japanese Tea Ceremony (Japan):**
   The Japanese tea ceremony, known as chanoyu or chado, is a highly ritualized practice that dates back to the 9th century. Rooted in Zen Buddhism, the tea ceremony emphasizes harmony, respect, and mindfulness. Participants gather in a traditional tea room, where a trained tea master prepares and serves matcha, a powdered green tea, using precise movements and gestures. The ceremony typically includes the sharing of sweets and quiet contemplation, creating a serene and meditative atmosphere.

2. **English Afternoon Tea (United Kingdom):**
   Afternoon tea is a quintessential English tradition that dates back to the 19th century. Originally introduced by Anna, the Duchess of Bedford, as a way to stave off hunger between meals, afternoon tea has evolved into a beloved social ritual enjoyed by people of all ages. Traditional afternoon tea features a selection of finger sandwiches, scones with clotted cream and jam, and an assortment of cakes and pastries, served alongside a pot of freshly brewed black tea.

3. Moroccan Mint Tea (Morocco):

Moroccan mint tea, or "atay," is a symbol of hospitality and friendship in Moroccan culture. This sweet and fragrant tea is made by steeping green tea leaves with fresh mint leaves and sugar, resulting in a refreshing and aromatic brew. Moroccan mint tea is traditionally served in small glasses with a flourish, as the tea is poured from a height to create a frothy foam. It is often enjoyed throughout the day and is an integral part of social gatherings and celebrations in Morocco.

Coffee:

1. Italian Espresso (Italy):

Espresso is the foundation of Italian coffee culture and is enjoyed by millions of Italians each day. Made by forcing hot water through finely ground coffee beans under high pressure, espresso is served in small, concentrated shots known as "caffè." Italians take their espresso seriously and often enjoy it standing at a bustling coffee bar, where they can quickly savor the rich, bold flavor and aromatic crema before continuing with their day.

2. Turkish Coffee (Turkey):

Turkish coffee, or "Türk kahvesi," is a traditional method of brewing coffee that dates back centuries. Finely ground coffee beans are simmered in water with sugar in a special pot called a cezve, resulting in a strong, thick brew with a layer of sediment at the bottom. Turkish coffee is typically served in small cups alongside a glass of water and a piece of Turkish delight. It is enjoyed leisurely as part of social gatherings and is often accompanied by lively conversation and storytelling.

3. Ethiopian Coffee Ceremony (Ethiopia):

The Ethiopian coffee ceremony, known as "buna," is a time-honored tradition that celebrates the importance of coffee in Ethiopian culture. The ceremony begins with the roasting of green coffee beans over an open flame, filling the air with the aroma of freshly roasted coffee. The roasted beans are then ground by hand and brewed in a traditional clay pot called a "jebena." The coffee is served in small cups, and the ceremony is a symbol of hospitality, friendship, and community bonding in Ethiopian culture.

Global Cuisine: Fusion and Cross-Cultural Influences

One of the most fascinating aspects of culinary exploration is the way in which different cultures and cuisines come together, resulting in fusion dishes that blend flavors, techniques, and ingredients from diverse culinary traditions. Whether through historical trade routes, migration patterns, or creative experimentation, the cross-pollination of food cultures has given rise to a rich tapestry of global cuisine that reflects the interconnectedness of our world. Here are some examples of fusion and cross-cultural influences in global cuisine:

1. **Peruvian-Japanese Cuisine (Nikkei Cuisine):**
   Nikkei cuisine is a unique fusion of Peruvian and Japanese culinary traditions that originated in Peru in the late 19th century with the arrival of Japanese immigrants. This fusion cuisine combines the delicate flavors and precise techniques of Japanese cooking with the vibrant ingredients and bold flavors of Peruvian cuisine. Iconic dishes of Nikkei cuisine include tiradito (a Peruvian-style sashimi), ceviche with soy sauce and ginger, and sushi rolls filled with Peruvian ingredients such as avocado and rocoto peppers.

2. **Tex-Mex Cuisine (United States):**
   Tex-Mex cuisine is a fusion of Texan and Mexican culinary traditions that developed along the border region of Texas and Mexico. This vibrant and flavorful cuisine blends elements of traditional Mexican cooking with Texan ingredients and cooking techniques, resulting in dishes such as chili con carne, nachos, fajitas, and Tex-Mex enchiladas. Tex-Mex cuisine has become immensely popular throughout the United States and has influenced American food culture on a national scale.

3. **Indo-Chinese Cuisine (India):**
   Indo-Chinese cuisine is a fusion of Indian and Chinese culinary traditions that emerged in the Indian subcontinent during the late 19th and early 20th centuries with the arrival of Chinese immigrants. This

unique cuisine combines Indian spices and cooking methods with Chinese ingredients and flavors, resulting in dishes such as chili chicken, hakka noodles, manchurian cauliflower, and sweet and sour vegetables. Indo-Chinese cuisine is immensely popular in India and has become a staple of street food culture in cities across the country.

4. Fusion Cuisine in Australia:

Australia's multicultural society has given rise to a diverse array of fusion cuisines that blend elements of Indigenous, European, Asian, and Middle Eastern culinary traditions. Examples include modern Australian cuisine, which combines Indigenous ingredients and cooking techniques with European influences, and Mod-Oz cuisine, which fuses Australian produce with Asian flavors and techniques. Other notable examples of fusion cuisine in Australia include Thai-Australian, Vietnamese-Australian, and Lebanese-Australian dishes.

5. Caribbean-Jewish Cuisine (Jewban):

Jewban cuisine is a fusion of Caribbean and Jewish culinary traditions that developed among Jewish communities in the Caribbean region, particularly in Cuba and Jamaica. This unique fusion cuisine combines Jewish dietary laws and traditional Caribbean ingredients and flavors, resulting in dishes such as matzo ball soup with plantains, jerk chicken latkes, and gefilte fish with mango salsa. Jewban cuisine reflects the cultural diversity and culinary creativity of Caribbean Jewish communities.

Unusual Eating Habits and Dining Etiquette

Across different cultures, dining customs and eating habits can vary significantly, reflecting unique traditions, social norms, and cultural values. While some practices may seem unusual or unfamiliar to outsiders, they often hold deep cultural significance and play an integral role in social interactions and communal gatherings. Here are some examples of unusual eating habits and dining etiquette from around the world:

1. Eating with Hands (Various Cultures):

In many cultures, eating with hands is not only common but also preferred over utensils. From Indian cuisine, where dishes like biryani and curry are traditionally enjoyed by hand, to Ethiopian cuisine, where injera (a spongy flatbread) is used to scoop up stews and salads, eating with hands is considered a tactile and sensory experience that enhances the enjoyment of food.

2. Communal Dining (Various Cultures):

Communal dining is a widespread practice in many cultures, where meals are shared among family members, friends, or even strangers. In Ethiopian culture, for example, injera is placed on a large platter, and various dishes are served on top for everyone to share. Similarly, in Korean culture, meals are often served family-style with multiple dishes placed in the center of the table for diners to help themselves.

3. No-Tipping Culture (Japan):

In Japan, tipping is not customary and can even be considered rude. Instead, exceptional service is expected as part of the overall dining experience. Japanese hospitality, or omotenashi, emphasizes the importance of anticipating the needs of guests and providing impeccable service without the expectation of monetary reward.

4. Burping as a Compliment (Tibet, China):

In Tibetan culture, burping after a meal is considered a sign of satisfaction and appreciation for the food. It is believed that burping demonstrates that one has enjoyed the meal and is a way of expressing gratitude to the host for their hospitality. Similarly, in some parts of China, burping after a meal is seen as a compliment to the chef.

5. Using Food as Utensils (Philippines):

In Filipino culture, it is common to use food items as utensils to eat other dishes. For example, kamayan-style dining involves eating with bare hands, using pieces of grilled meat or seafood to scoop up rice and vegetables. Similarly, lumpia (Filipino spring rolls) are often used to pick up adobo (marinated meat) or pancit (noodles), creating a dynamic and interactive dining experience.

6. Pouring Drinks for Others (South Korea):

In South Korean dining etiquette, it is customary for the youngest or most junior person at the table to pour drinks for their elders or seniors as a sign of respect. The act of pouring drinks, known as "sool-jung-rye," is accompanied by a polite bow and is seen as a gesture of deference and courtesy.

Chapter 9
Transportation
Marvels

Iconic Bridges Around the World

Bridges are not only essential transportation links but also iconic landmarks that symbolize human ingenuity, engineering prowess, and architectural beauty. From ancient stone structures to modern steel marvels, bridges connect communities, span natural obstacles, and serve as enduring symbols of human achievement. Here are some of the most iconic bridges from around the world:

1. Golden Gate Bridge (San Francisco, USA):

The Golden Gate Bridge is one of the most recognizable landmarks in the world and a symbol of San Francisco. Completed in 1937, this iconic suspension bridge spans the Golden Gate Strait, connecting the city of San Francisco to Marin County. With its distinctive orange color and Art Deco design, the Golden Gate Bridge stretches 2.7 kilometers (1.7 miles) across the bay, offering breathtaking views of the city skyline and the surrounding landscape.

2. Brooklyn Bridge (New York City, USA):

The Brooklyn Bridge is an iconic suspension bridge that spans the East River, connecting the boroughs of Manhattan and Brooklyn in New York City. Completed in 1883, the Brooklyn Bridge was the first steel-wire suspension bridge ever constructed and a marvel of 19th-century engineering. With its elegant Gothic-style towers and graceful arched cables, the Brooklyn Bridge is not only a vital transportation link but also a beloved symbol of New York City.

3. Tower Bridge (London, UK):

Tower Bridge is an iconic bascule and suspension bridge that crosses the River Thames in London. Completed in 1894, this magnificent bridge is renowned for its distinctive twin towers, Victorian Gothic architecture, and intricate bascule mechanism that allows the central span to be raised to accommodate passing ships. Tower Bridge has become an enduring symbol of London and a must-visit attraction for tourists from around the world.

4. Sydney Harbour Bridge (Sydney, Australia):

The Sydney Harbour Bridge is an iconic steel through-arch bridge that spans Sydney Harbour, connecting the central business district with the

North Shore. Completed in 1932, this monumental structure is the tallest steel arch bridge in the world and a beloved symbol of Sydney. Affectionately known as the "Coathanger" due to its distinctive shape, the Sydney Harbour Bridge is not only a vital transportation link but also a popular tourist attraction, offering panoramic views of the harbor and the Sydney Opera House.

5. **Akashi Kaikyō Bridge (Hyogo, Japan):**

The Akashi Kaikyō Bridge, also known as the Pearl Bridge, is the longest suspension bridge in the world, spanning the Akashi Strait between the city of Kobe and Awaji Island in Japan. Completed in 1998, this engineering marvel stretches 3,911 meters (12,831 feet) in length and features three towers that support the massive steel cables. The Akashi Kaikyō Bridge is admired for its sleek design, resilience against earthquakes and typhoons, and stunning views of the surrounding coastline.

Unusual Modes of Transportation

While cars, trains, and airplanes are the most common forms of transportation, there are many unconventional and fascinating modes of getting from point A to point B around the world. These unusual methods of transportation offer unique experiences and insights into different cultures, landscapes, and lifestyles. Here are some examples of unusual modes of transportation from various corners of the globe:

1. **Yak Riding (Himalayas, Tibet, and Mongolia):**

In the remote regions of the Himalayas, Tibet, and Mongolia, yaks are used as a primary mode of transportation in rugged terrain where vehicles cannot access. Yaks are sturdy, sure-footed animals that are well-suited for traversing steep mountain paths and high-altitude landscapes. Local nomadic communities rely on yaks for carrying goods, transporting supplies, and even providing rides for travelers seeking to explore the remote corners of the Himalayan region.

2. **Sled Dogs (Arctic and Subarctic Regions):**

In the Arctic and Subarctic regions, where harsh winter conditions prevail, sled dogs have long been used as a traditional mode of transportation. Teams of huskies or other breeds of working dogs are harnessed to sleds or sledges and pulled across snow-covered terrain. Sled dog races, such as the Iditarod in Alaska and the Finnmarksløpet in Norway, showcase the speed, endurance, and teamwork of these remarkable canine athletes.

3. Pedicabs (Southeast Asia and South Asia):

Pedicabs, also known as cycle rickshaws or trishaws, are a common mode of transportation in cities and towns across Southeast Asia and South Asia. These human-powered vehicles consist of a bicycle with a sidecar or trailer attached, where passengers sit while being pedaled by the driver. Pedicabs provide a convenient and environmentally friendly way to navigate crowded urban streets and narrow alleyways, offering a unique perspective on local life and culture.

4. Sandboarding (Desert Regions):

In desert regions such as the Sahara Desert in North Africa and the Atacama Desert in South America, sandboarding has become a popular recreational activity and mode of transportation. Similar to snowboarding, sandboarding involves riding down sand dunes on a specially designed board, using gravity to glide over the sandy terrain. Sandboarding tours and competitions attract thrill-seekers and adventure enthusiasts from around the world, providing an adrenaline-pumping experience in the heart of the desert.

5. Floating Villages (Tonle Sap Lake, Cambodia):

In Cambodia, the Tonle Sap Lake is home to a network of floating villages where residents live in houses built on stilts or floating platforms. Boat transportation is the primary mode of getting around in these unique communities, with residents using wooden boats or canoes to navigate the waterways for fishing, transportation, and commerce. Visiting the floating villages offers a glimpse into a way of life that is intimately connected to the rhythms of the lake and its surrounding wetlands.

6. Bamboo Trains (Battambang, Cambodia):

In the Cambodian city of Battambang, bamboo trains, known as "norries," are a popular and unconventional mode of transportation. These makeshift trains consist of a bamboo platform mounted on wheels and powered by a small engine. Passengers sit or stand on the platform as it travels along the railway tracks, providing a fast and affordable way to explore the countryside and visit nearby villages.

Spectacular Highways and Roads

Around the world, highways and roads are more than just transportation routes; they are engineering marvels that traverse breathtaking landscapes, connect remote regions, and offer unforgettable journeys for travelers. From winding mountain passes to coastal highways with panoramic ocean views, these spectacular roads showcase the beauty of the natural world while providing access to some of the most remote and picturesque destinations. Here are some examples of spectacular highways and roads from around the globe:

1. Atlantic Road (Norway):
The Atlantic Road, also known as Atlanterhavsveien, is a scenic highway that winds its way along the rugged coastline of western Norway. Spanning a series of small islands and archipelagos, the Atlantic Road offers breathtaking views of the Norwegian Sea and the dramatic coastal landscape. The road features several iconic bridges, including the Storseisundet Bridge, which appears to curve gracefully over the water, creating a stunning visual spectacle.

2. Great Ocean Road (Australia):
The Great Ocean Road is one of the most scenic coastal drives in the world, stretching along the southeastern coast of Australia between the cities of Torquay and Allansford. This iconic road hugs the cliffs of the Victorian coastline, offering panoramic views of the Southern Ocean, pristine beaches, and dramatic rock formations such as the Twelve Apostles. The Great Ocean Road is not only a popular tourist attraction but also a designated National Heritage site that showcases the natural beauty of Australia's coastline.

3. Transfagarasan Highway (Romania):
The Transfagarasan Highway is a breathtaking mountain road that winds its way through the Fagaras Mountains in central Romania. Built in the 1970s as a strategic military route, this spectacular highway

traverses rugged terrain, steep inclines, and dramatic hairpin bends, reaching an elevation of over 2,000 meters (6,500 feet). The Transfagarasan Highway offers stunning views of alpine meadows, glacial lakes, and the imposing peaks of the Carpathian Mountains.

4. Highway 1 (California, USA):

Highway 1, also known as the Pacific Coast Highway, is a legendary scenic route that hugs the rugged coastline of California, stretching from the northern border with Oregon to the southern border with Mexico. This iconic highway offers jaw-dropping views of the Pacific Ocean, towering cliffs, sandy beaches, and picturesque seaside towns such as Big Sur and Monterey. Highway 1 is renowned for its dramatic coastal scenery and is considered one of the most scenic drives in the United States.

5. Grossglockner High Alpine Road (Austria):

The Grossglockner High Alpine Road, or Großglockner-Hochalpenstraße, is a stunning mountain pass road that winds its way through the Austrian Alps, offering unparalleled views of snow-capped peaks, glacial valleys, and alpine meadows. Climbing to an elevation of over 2,500 meters (8,200 feet), this scenic road features numerous switchbacks, tunnels, and panoramic viewpoints that showcase the natural beauty of the Hohe Tauern National Park.

Historic and Scenic Rail Journeys

Rail travel has long been celebrated for its ability to traverse diverse landscapes, connect distant destinations, and provide passengers with unforgettable experiences. From historic steam trains to modern luxury trains, rail journeys offer a unique perspective on the world's most scenic and culturally rich regions. Here are some of the most iconic and historic rail journeys from around the globe:

1. The Orient Express (Europe):

The Orient Express is perhaps the most legendary and iconic train journey in history. Originally launched in 1883, the Orient Express connected Paris to Istanbul, passing through cities such as Vienna, Budapest, and Bucharest. Renowned for its luxurious accommodations, fine dining, and romantic ambiance, the Orient Express captured the imagination of travelers and inspired countless novels, films, and cultural references. While the original Orient Express route no longer operates in its entirety, several luxury train companies offer recreated journeys that evoke the elegance and glamour of the golden age of rail travel.

2. The Trans-Siberian Railway (Russia):

The Trans-Siberian Railway is the longest continuous railway line in the world, spanning over 9,000 kilometers (5,600 miles) from Moscow to Vladivostok. Built between 1891 and 1916, this historic railway traverses the vast expanse of Russia, crossing eight time zones and passing through diverse landscapes ranging from dense forests to barren steppes. The Trans-Siberian Railway offers passengers the opportunity to experience the beauty and grandeur of Siberia, as well as the rich cultural heritage of the cities and towns along the route.

3. The Glacier Express (Switzerland):

The Glacier Express is one of the most scenic train journeys in the world, offering breathtaking view of the Swiss Alps. Running between the mountain resorts of Zermatt and St. Moritz, the Glacier Express traverses spectacular mountain passes, crosses deep valleys, and passes through charming alpine villages. The journey takes approximately eight hours, during which passengers can marvel at the stunning scenery from panoramic windows and enjoy gourmet meals served onboard.

4. The Ghan (Australia):

The Ghan is an iconic rail journey that traverses the heart of Australia, from Adelaide in the south to Darwin in the north. Covering a distance of over 2,979 kilometers (1,851 miles), The Ghan crosses the vast Outback, passing through remote desert landscapes, ancient Indigenous lands, and historic gold rush towns. Named after the Afghan camel drivers who once traversed the region, The Ghan offers passengers a glimpse into Australia's rich history, culture, and natural beauty.

5. The Rocky Mountaineer (Canada):

The Rocky Mountaineer is a luxury train journey that winds its way through the stunning landscapes of the Canadian Rockies, from Vancouver to Banff, Jasper, or Calgary. This scenic route offers panoramic views of snow-capped mountains, turquoise lakes, and deep river canyons as it travels through British Columbia and Alberta. Passengers can choose from a variety of routes and travel classes, including GoldLeaf Service, which features glass-domed observation cars and gourmet dining.

Innovative Airports and Aviation Facts

Airports are vital hubs of global transportation, serving as gateways to cities, regions, and countries around the world. Over the years, airports have evolved from simple airstrips to complex transportation hubs equipped with state-of-the-art technology, innovative design features, and sustainable practices. Here are some fascinating facts about innovative airports and aviation:

1. **Singapore Changi Airport (Singapore):**
   Singapore Changi Airport consistently ranks among the best airports in the world for its exceptional facilities, efficiency, and passenger experience. The airport features unique amenities such as the Butterfly Garden, a rooftop swimming pool, and the world's tallest indoor waterfall, known as the Rain Vortex. Changi Airport is also renowned for its efficiency, with one of the shortest average waiting times for security and immigration clearance.

2. **Hamad International Airport (Qatar):**
   Hamad International Airport in Doha, Qatar, is one of the most innovative airports in the Middle East, known for its cutting-edge design and state-of-the-art facilities. The airport features a stunning passenger terminal inspired by the shape of a desert rose, as well as a range of luxury amenities, including a hotel with a swimming pool overlooking the runway and an art gallery showcasing contemporary Qatari art.

3. **Incheon International Airport (South Korea):**

Incheon International Airport in Seoul, South Korea, is renowned for its efficiency, cleanliness, and advanced technology. The airport features a fully automated baggage handling system, which can process over 19,000 bags per hour, as well as biometric immigration gates that use facial recognition technology to expedite passenger clearance. Incheon Airport also boasts a range of cultural amenities, including a traditional Korean cultural experience center and a museum showcasing Korean art and history.

4. The Jet Age and Supersonic Travel:

The advent of the Jet Age in the 1950s revolutionized air travel, making it faster, safer, and more accessible to the masses. Commercial jetliners such as the Boeing 707 and the Douglas DC-8 ushered in a new era of long-distance travel, shrinking the world and connecting continents in a matter of hours. In the 1960s and 1970s, supersonic passenger aircraft such as the Concorde and the Tupolev Tu-144 offered even greater speed and luxury, with transatlantic flights taking less than half the time of conventional aircraft.

5. Green Airports and Sustainable Practices:

With growing awareness of environmental issues, many airports around the world are implementing sustainable practices to reduce their carbon footprint and minimize environmental impact. This includes initiatives such as energy-efficient lighting systems, solar panels for power generation, rainwater harvesting, and waste recycling programs. Some airports are also investing in alternative fuels and electric ground vehicles to reduce emissions and promote cleaner air travel.

6. Future of Aviation: Urban Air Mobility:

The future of aviation holds exciting possibilities with the development of urban air mobility (UAM) technologies, including electric vertical takeoff and landing (eVTOL) aircraft and autonomous air taxis. These innovative aircraft promise to revolutionize urban transportation by providing fast, efficient, and environmentally friendly aerial mobility solutions for passengers and cargo in congested city environments.

Chapter 10
Biodiversity Hotspots and Unique Wildlife

Hotspots of Biodiversity: Rainforests, Coral Reefs, and More

Biodiversity hotspots are regions of exceptional ecological richness and diversity, harboring a wide variety of plant and animal species found nowhere else on Earth. These areas are characterized by high levels of endemism, meaning that a significant proportion of species are unique to the region. From lush rainforests to vibrant coral reefs, biodiversity hotspots play a crucial role in supporting global biodiversity and providing essential ecosystem services. Here are some of the most iconic hotspots of biodiversity:

1. Tropical Rainforests:

Tropical rainforests are among the most biodiverse ecosystems on Earth, containing a staggering array of plant and animal species. Found near the equator in regions such as the Amazon Basin in South America, the Congo Basin in Central Africa, and the islands of Southeast Asia, tropical rainforests are characterized by dense vegetation, high levels of rainfall, and year-round warmth. These ecosystems support a wide variety of species, including jaguars, orangutans, toucans, and countless species of birds, insects, and plants.

2. Coral Reefs:

Coral reefs are underwater ecosystems formed by colonies of tiny marine organisms known as coral polyps. Found in shallow, warm waters around the world, coral reefs are home to a diverse array of marine life, including colorful fish, sea turtles, sharks, and dolphins. Coral reefs provide vital habitat for thousands of species and contribute to the health and resilience of marine ecosystems. However, coral reefs are increasingly threatened by factors such as climate change, ocean acidification, and overfishing, putting many species at risk of extinction.

3. Mediterranean Basin:

The Mediterranean Basin is a biodiversity hotspot characterized by its unique climate, geography, and rich cultural heritage. Stretching from southern Europe to North Africa and the Middle East, the Mediterranean Basin is home to a remarkable variety of plant and animal species, including iconic species such as the Mediterranean monk seal, the European green crab, and the Corsican swallowtail butterfly. However, the region faces numerous threats, including habitat loss, pollution, and climate change, putting many species at risk of extinction.

4. Madagascar:

Madagascar is a biodiversity hotspot renowned for its extraordinary array of unique plant and animal species found nowhere else on Earth. As an isolated island off the coast of Africa, Madagascar has evolved its own distinct ecosystems, including lush rainforests, dry deciduous forests, and spiny desert habitats. The island is home to iconic species such as the lemurs, chameleons, and baobab trees, as well as countless other endemic species of plants and animals. However, Madagascar's biodiversity is threatened by habitat loss, deforestation, and illegal wildlife trade, making conservation efforts crucial for the survival of its unique ecosystems.

5. Western Ghats:

The Western Ghats mountain range in India is a biodiversity hotspot renowned for its rich biological diversity and unique ecosystems. Stretching along the western coast of India, the Western Ghats are home to thousands of plant and animal species, including many endemic species found nowhere else on Earth. The region's diverse habitats include tropical rainforests, montane grasslands, and freshwater wetlands, providing vital habitat for species such as the Bengal tiger, the Asian elephant, and the lion-tailed macaque. However, the Western Ghats face numerous threats, including habitat loss, deforestation, and fragmentation, highlighting the need for conservation efforts to protect its unique biodiversity.

Unusual Creatures: From Axolotls to Narwhals

The natural world is filled with an astonishing diversity of life, ranging from the familiar to the utterly bizarre. From mysterious deep-sea creatures to peculiar land-dwellers, the animal kingdom is home to a myriad of fascinating species that captivate the imagination. Here are some examples of unusual creatures that inhabit different ecosystems around the world:

1. Axolotl (Ambystoma mexicanum):

The axolotl is a unique amphibian native to the ancient lake complex of Xochimilco in Mexico City. Known for its striking appearance and remarkable regenerative abilities, the axolotl is sometimes referred to as the "Mexican walking fish" despite being a salamander rather than a fish. One of the most notable features of the axolotl is its ability to regenerate lost limbs, organs, and even parts of its brain, making it a subject of scientific interest and a popular pet in the aquarium trade.

2. Narwhal (Monodon monoceros):

The narwhal is a fascinating Arctic whale known for its long, spiral tusk that protrudes from its head. Found in the icy waters of the Arctic Ocean, narwhals are often referred to as the "unicorns of the sea" due to their distinctive tusks, which can grow up to 10 feet in length. While the exact purpose of the narwhal's tusk remains a subject of debate among scientists, it is believed to play a role in communication, navigation, and mating displays.

3. Aye-Aye (Daubentonia madagascariensis):

The aye-aye is a peculiar primate found only on the island of Madagascar. With its large eyes, bushy tail, and elongated middle finger, the aye-aye has a distinctive appearance that sets it apart from other lemurs. The aye-aye is renowned for its unique foraging behavior, using its specialized middle finger to tap on trees and locate hidden insect larvae, which it then extracts using its slender, rodent-like incisors.

4. Blobfish (Psychrolutes marcidus):

The blobfish is a deep-sea fish that inhabits the cold, high-pressure waters of the deep ocean. Known for its gelatinous appearance and droopy, sagging features, the blobfish has earned the title of "world's ugliest animal" in popular culture. Despite its unappealing appearance, the blobfish is perfectly adapted to its deep-sea environment, with a low-density body that allows it to float effortlessly above the seabed while conserving energy.

5. Okapi (Okapia johnstoni):

The okapi is a peculiar mammal native to the dense rainforests of the Democratic Republic of the Congo in Central Africa. Resembling a cross between a giraffe and a zebra, the okapi has a sleek, chestnut-brown coat with white stripes on its legs and hindquarters. Despite its striking appearance, the okapi remained unknown to Western science until the late 19th century, when it was discovered by British explorers. Today, the okapi is listed as an endangered species due to habitat loss and poaching.

6. Platypus (Ornithorhynchus anatinus):

The platypus is a truly unique mammal found in freshwater habitats along the eastern coast of Australia. With its duck-like bill, webbed feet, and beaver-like tail, the platypus is one of the most bizarre creatures in the animal kingdom. The platypus is also one of only a few mammals that lay eggs, making it a fascinating subject of scientific study and a symbol of Australia's rich biodiversity.

Endangered Species and Conservation Efforts

Across the globe, countless species are teetering on the brink of extinction due to habitat loss, poaching, climate change, and other human-induced threats. Conservation efforts are crucial for protecting these vulnerable species and preserving Earth's rich biodiversity for future generations. Here are some examples of endangered species and the conservation efforts aimed at their protection:

1. Sumatran Tiger (Panthera tigris sumatrae):

The Sumatran tiger is a critically endangered subspecies of tiger found only on the Indonesian island of Sumatra. With fewer than 400 individuals remaining in the wild, the Sumatran tiger is threatened by habitat loss due to deforestation, as well as poaching for their valuable body parts. Conservation efforts to protect the Sumatran tiger include establishing protected areas, combating illegal poaching and logging, and promoting sustainable land-use practices.

2. Amur Leopard (Panthera pardus orientalis):

The Amur leopard is one of the most endangered big cats in the world, with fewer than 100 individuals remaining in the wild. Native to the temperate forests of the Russian Far East, the Amur leopard is threatened by habitat loss, poaching, and human-wildlife conflict. Conservation efforts to save the Amur leopard include establishing protected areas, implementing anti-poaching measures, and promoting community-based conservation initiatives.

3. Vaquita (Phocoena sinus):

The vaquita is a critically endangered species of porpoise found only in the northern Gulf of California, Mexico. With fewer than 10 individuals remaining, the vaquita is the most endangered cetacean species in the world. The primary threat to the vaquita is accidental entanglement in illegal gillnets used for fishing the endangered totoaba fish. Conservation efforts to save the vaquita include banning the use of gillnets in its habitat, enforcing marine protected areas, and supporting alternative livelihoods for local fishing communities.

4. Javan Rhino (Rhinoceros sondaicus):

The Javan rhinoceros is one of the rarest and most endangered large mammals on Earth, with fewer than 80 individuals remaining in the wild. Found only on the Indonesian island of Java, the Javan rhino is threatened by habitat loss, poaching, and natural disasters such as volcanic eruptions and tsunamis. Conservation efforts to protect the Javan rhino include establishing protected areas, translocating individuals to safer habitats, and implementing anti-poaching patrols.

5. Hawksbill Turtle (Eretmochelys imbricata):

The hawksbill turtle is a critically endangered species of sea turtle found in tropical and subtropical oceans around the world. Hawksbill turtles are threatened by habitat loss, pollution, climate change, and illegal poaching for their prized shell, which is used to make jewelry and ornaments. Conservation efforts to protect hawksbill turtles include establishing marine protected areas, reducing plastic pollution, and monitoring nesting beaches to prevent poaching and disturbance.

Wildlife Migrations: Nature's Grand Journeys

Every year, millions of animals embark on epic migrations across vast distances in search of food, breeding grounds, or favorable climates.

These incredible journeys showcase the remarkable adaptations and resilience of wildlife as they navigate diverse landscapes and overcome formidable challenges. From the Serengeti's Great Migration to the Arctic tern's annual round-trip migration, here are some examples of nature's grandest migrations:

1. The Great Migration (East Africa):
The Great Migration is one of the most iconic wildlife spectacles on Earth, involving millions of wildebeest, zebras, and other ungulates moving in search of fresh grazing pastures in the Serengeti ecosystem of Tanzania and the Maasai Mara National Reserve in Kenya. This annual migration spans over 1,800 miles (2,900 kilometers) and is driven by seasonal rainfall patterns, with the animals following the lush grasslands in a perpetual cycle of movement. The migration is not only a breathtaking display of natural beauty but also a crucial ecological event that sustains local predator populations and shapes the landscape.

2. Monarch Butterfly Migration (North America):
The monarch butterfly migration is one of the most remarkable insect migrations in the world, with millions of butterflies traveling thousands of miles between their breeding grounds in North America and their overwintering sites in central Mexico. This incredible journey spans multiple generations, as successive generations of monarch butterflies make their way north in the spring and south in the fall. The monarch butterfly migration is threatened by habitat loss, climate change, and pesticide use, highlighting the need for conservation efforts to protect this iconic species.

3. Arctic Tern Migration (Global):
The Arctic tern holds the record for the longest migration of any bird species, traveling an astonishing 71,000 kilometers (44,000 miles) round-trip between its breeding grounds in the Arctic and its wintering grounds in the Antarctic. This incredible journey takes the Arctic tern through every ocean and across all continents, making it one of the most well-traveled species on Earth. The Arctic tern's migration is driven by the need to take advantage of abundant food resources in both polar regions and to avoid harsh winter conditions in the Arctic.

4. Blue Whale Migration (Global):

The blue whale, the largest animal on Earth, undertakes seasonal migrations between its feeding grounds in cold, nutrient-rich polar waters and its breeding and calving grounds in warmer, more temperate waters. These migrations can span thousands of miles and often coincide with the movement of prey species such as krill. While the exact routes of blue whale migrations vary by population, these majestic creatures can be found in every ocean on the planet, making them a truly global species.

5. Caribou Migration (North America):

Caribou, also known as reindeer in Eurasia, undertake one of the longest overland migrations of any terrestrial mammal, traveling hundreds or even thousands of miles between their summer and winter ranges in the Arctic and subarctic regions of North America and Eurasia. These migrations are driven by the need to find suitable food sources and avoid harsh winter conditions, and they play a crucial role in shaping the ecology of northern ecosystems.

The World's Strangest and Rarest Animals

The diversity of life on Earth never ceases to amaze, and some species stand out for their extraordinary appearance, behavior, or rarity. From elusive deep-sea creatures to bizarre insects found in remote rainforests, the world is home to an array of strange and rare animals that capture the imagination. Here are some examples of the world's strangest and rarest animals:

1. Saola (Pseudoryx nghetinhensis):

The saola, also known as the "Asian unicorn," is a rare and elusive mammal native to the forests of Vietnam and Laos. With its long, slender horns and striking white facial markings, the saola resembles a mythical creature straight out of a fairy tale. First discovered in 1992, the saola is one of the most enigmatic and least understood large mammals in the world. Threatened by habitat loss, hunting, and snaring, the saola is listed as critically endangered, with fewer than 100 individuals believed to remain in the wild.

2. Pangolin:

Pangolins are a group of eight species of nocturnal mammals native to Africa and Asia. Covered in scales made of keratin, pangolins are often referred to as "scaly anteaters" and are highly prized for their meat and scales in traditional Chinese medicine. All eight species of pangolin are listed as threatened with extinction, with some species, such as the Chinese pangolin and the Sunda pangolin, classified as critically endangered due to poaching and habitat loss.

3. Aye-Aye (Daubentonia madagascariensis):

The aye-aye is a peculiar primate found only on the island of Madagascar. With its large eyes, bushy tail, and elongated middle finger, the aye-aye has a distinctive appearance that sets it apart from other lemurs. The aye-aye is renowned for its unique foraging behavior, using its specialized middle finger to tap on trees and locate hidden insect larvae, which it then extracts using its slender, rodent-like incisors.

4. Axolotl (Ambystoma mexicanum):

The axolotl is a unique amphibian native to the ancient lake complex of Xochimilco in Mexico City. Known for its striking appearance and remarkable regenerative abilities, the axolotl is sometimes referred to as the "Mexican walking fish" despite being a salamander rather than a fish. One of the most notable features of the axolotl is its ability to regenerate lost limbs, organs, and even parts of its brain, making it a subject of scientific interest and a popular pet in the aquarium trade.

5. Blobfish (Psychrolutes marcidus):

The blobfish is a deep-sea fish that inhabits the cold, high-pressure waters of the deep ocean. Known for its gelatinous appearance and droopy, sagging features, the blobfish has earned the title of "world's ugliest animal" in popular culture. Despite its unappealing appearance, the blobfish is perfectly adapted to its deep-sea environment, with a low-density body that allows it to float effortlessly above the seabed while conserving energy.

6. Okapi (Okapia johnstoni):

The okapi is a peculiar mammal native to the dense rainforests of the Democratic Republic of the Congo in Central Africa. Resembling a cross between a giraffe and a zebra, the okapi has a sleek, chestnut-brown coat with white stripes on its legs and hindquarters. Despite its striking appearance, the okapi remained unknown to Western science until the late 19th century, when it was discovered by British explorers. Today, the okapi is listed as an endangered species due to habitat loss and poaching.

Chapter 11
Cultural Practices and Traditions

Wedding Customs Around the Globe

Weddings are celebrated in diverse ways across cultures, each reflecting the unique traditions, beliefs, and customs of the communities involved. From elaborate ceremonies steeped in tradition to modern interpretations influenced by globalization, weddings offer a fascinating glimpse into the cultural fabric of societies around the world. Here are some examples of wedding customs from different regions:

1. India:

In India, weddings are colorful and elaborate affairs that often span several days and involve numerous rituals and ceremonies. One common tradition is the Mehendi ceremony, where intricate henna designs are applied to the hands and feet of the bride and other female relatives. Another important ritual is the Saptapadi, or seven steps, where the bride and groom take seven symbolic steps together to signify their lifelong commitment to each other.

2. China:

Traditional Chinese weddings often feature symbolic rituals that date back centuries. One such ritual is the Tea Ceremony, where the bride and groom serve tea to their parents and other relatives as a gesture of respect and gratitude. Red is considered a lucky color in Chinese culture, so it is often incorporated into wedding decorations, attire, and gifts. The Double Happiness symbol, representing marital bliss, is also commonly seen at Chinese weddings.

3. Japan:

Japanese weddings blend traditional Shinto rituals with modern customs influenced by Western culture. One popular tradition is the exchange of sake cups, known as san-san-kudo, where the bride and groom take three sips each from three cups of sake to symbolize their union. Another important custom is the presentation of the wedding kimonos, where the bride and groom wear traditional attire during the ceremony.

4. Nigeria:

Nigerian weddings are vibrant and lively celebrations that showcase
the rich cultural heritage of the country's diverse ethnic groups. One
common tradition is the spraying of money, where guests shower the
bride and groom with cash as a symbol of prosperity and good fortune.
Another important custom is the breaking of the kola nut, which is
performed by the couple's parents to symbolize unity and hospitality.

5. **Scotland:**
   Scottish weddings often feature traditional elements such as bagpipe
music, kilts, and the exchange of tartan sashes or scarves. One unique
Scottish custom is the Quaich ceremony, where the bride and groom
drink from a two-handled cup to symbolize their shared future
together. Another important tradition is the handfasting ceremony,
where the couple's hands are bound together with a ribbon or cord to
symbolize their union.

6. **Mexico:**
   Mexican weddings are festive occasions filled with music, dancing,
and traditional foods. One popular tradition is the Lazo ceremony,
where the couple is draped with a floral garland or rosary in the shape
of a figure eight to symbolize their eternal bond. Another important
custom is the presentation of the arras, or coins, which are blessed by
the priest and given to the bride as a symbol of the groom's
commitment to providing for their future.

Coming-of-Age Rituals and Initiations

Throughout history and across cultures, societies have marked the
transition from childhood to adulthood with special rituals and
ceremonies. These coming-of-age rituals serve as important milestones
in a person's life, signifying their readiness to take on adult
responsibilities and roles within their community. From elaborate
ceremonies steeped in tradition to modern interpretations influenced
by globalization, coming-of-age rituals offer a fascinating glimpse into
the cultural values and beliefs of different societies. Here are some
examples of coming-of-age rituals and initiations from around the
world:

1. Bar and Bat Mitzvah (Judaism):

In the Jewish tradition, the Bar Mitzvah (for boys) and Bat Mitzvah (for girls) ceremonies mark the transition from childhood to adulthood. Typically held around the age of 13, these ceremonies involve the young person reading from the Torah and leading prayers in front of their community. The Bar and Bat Mitzvah signify the individual's acceptance of their religious obligations and responsibilities as an adult member of the Jewish community.

2. Quinceañera (Latin America):

The Quinceañera is a traditional coming-of-age celebration for girls in many Latin American countries, particularly Mexico and parts of Central America. Celebrated on a girl's fifteenth birthday, the Quinceañera marks her transition from childhood to womanhood. The celebration often includes a religious ceremony, a lavish party with family and friends, and symbolic rituals such as the presentation of a tiara and scepter to the birthday girl.

3. Seijin-no-Hi (Japan):

Seijin-no-Hi, or Coming of Age Day, is a Japanese holiday held annually on the second Monday of January to celebrate young people who have reached the age of 20, the legal age of adulthood in Japan. On this day, young adults dress in traditional kimono attire and attend ceremonies and festivities organized by local government authorities. Seijin-no-Hi is a time for young people to reflect on their responsibilities as adults and to celebrate their transition to adulthood with friends and family.

4. Sun Dance (Native American Tribes):

The Sun Dance is a sacred ritual practiced by many Native American tribes, including the Lakota, Cheyenne, and Crow. Typically held in the summer months, the Sun Dance involves fasting, prayer, and ritualistic dances performed around a central pole adorned with symbolic items such as eagle feathers and buffalo skulls. The Sun Dance is a rite of passage for young men seeking spiritual guidance and strength, as well as a time for community bonding and renewal.

5. Initiation Ceremonies (African Cultures):

Many African cultures have traditional initiation ceremonies that mark the transition from childhood to adulthood for both boys and girls. These ceremonies often involve rituals such as circumcision, scarification, and seclusion, as well as teachings on cultural traditions, morals, and values. Initiation ceremonies vary widely across different African cultures, but they all serve to prepare young people for their roles as adults within their communities.

6. Sweet Sixteen (United States):
In the United States, the Sweet Sixteen party is a popular coming-of-age celebration for teenage girls. Similar to the Quinceañera, the Sweet Sixteen typically involves a lavish party with family and friends to celebrate the girl's sixteenth birthday and mark her transition to young adulthood. The celebration often includes music, dancing, and symbolic rituals such as the lighting of sixteen candles to represent important milestones in the girl's life.

Funeral Rites and Mourning Traditions

Funeral rites and mourning traditions vary widely across cultures, reflecting diverse beliefs, customs, and rituals associated with death and the afterlife. These practices play a crucial role in helping families and communities cope with loss, honor the deceased, and navigate the grieving process. From elaborate funeral ceremonies to unique mourning customs, funeral rites offer insights into the cultural values and beliefs of different societies. Here are some examples of funeral rites and mourning traditions from around the world:

1. Traditional Buddhist Funerals (Asia):
In many Asian cultures influenced by Buddhism, funeral rites typically involve elaborate rituals aimed at guiding the deceased's soul to the afterlife and providing comfort to the bereaved. Traditional Buddhist funerals often include chanting of sutras by monks, offerings of incense, flowers, and food, and the performance of merit-making activities such as almsgiving and donations to temples. Cremation is a common practice in many Buddhist cultures, although burial and sky burials are also observed in some regions.

2. Dia de los Muertos (Mexico):

Dia de los Muertos, or Day of the Dead, is a vibrant and colorful celebration observed in Mexico and other Latin American countries to honor deceased loved ones and celebrate their lives. Families create elaborate altars, or ofrendas, adorned with photographs, candles, flowers, and offerings of food and drink to welcome the spirits of the departed back to the earthly realm. The celebration often includes music, dancing, and parades, as well as visits to cemeteries to clean and decorate graves.

3. Irish Wake (Ireland):

In Ireland and other Celtic cultures, the wake is a traditional mourning ritual held after a person's death to allow family and friends to gather, pay their respects, and share stories and memories of the deceased. Historically, wakes were held in the home of the deceased, with the body laid out on a table or in a coffin surrounded by candles and mourners. The wake often continues throughout the night, with music, food, and drink provided to comfort the bereaved.

4. Sky Burial (Tibet):

In Tibetan Buddhism, sky burial, or jhator, is a traditional funerary practice in which the deceased's body is ritually dismembered and offered to birds of prey, typically vultures, as a form of almsgiving and compassion. Sky burial is based on the belief in the impermanence of the body and the transmigration of the soul, and it is seen as a way to facilitate the deceased's journey to the afterlife while benefiting other sentient beings.

5. Sitting Shiva (Judaism):

In the Jewish tradition, sitting Shiva is a period of mourning observed by the immediate family of the deceased for seven days following the funeral. During Shiva, mourners gather in the home of the deceased or another designated location to recite prayers, share memories, and receive visitors who come to offer condolences and support. Traditionally, mirrors are covered, and mourners refrain from wearing leather shoes and engaging in activities of leisure or pleasure as a sign of respect for the deceased.

6. Viking Funeral (Scandinavia):

In Norse mythology and Scandinavian folklore, the Viking funeral was a ceremonial practice in which the deceased's body was placed on a boat or ship, along with valuable possessions, weapons, and offerings, and set ablaze as it floated out to sea. The Viking funeral was believed to ensure a warrior's safe passage to Valhalla, the mythical hall of the slain, and to honor their bravery and achievements in life.

Traditional Clothing and Its Significance

Traditional clothing reflects the cultural identity, history, and values of a community, serving as a powerful symbol of heritage and belonging. Across the globe, diverse cultures have developed unique styles of dress that express their distinctiveness and celebrate their shared identity. From intricate ceremonial garments to everyday attire, traditional clothing plays a central role in preserving cultural heritage and fostering a sense of pride and connection among people. Here are some examples of traditional clothing and their significance in different cultures:

1. **Kimono (Japan):**
   The kimono is a traditional Japanese garment characterized by its long, straight-line silhouette, wide sleeves, and wrap-around style. Kimonos are often made from luxurious silk fabrics and adorned with elaborate patterns and motifs that reflect seasonal themes or auspicious symbols. Historically worn by both men and women, kimonos are associated with formal occasions such as weddings, tea ceremonies, and festivals, as well as everyday wear for special events.

2. **Sari (India):**
   The sari is a traditional garment worn by women in India, consisting of a long piece of fabric draped elegantly around the body, with one end draped over the shoulder and the other end wrapped around the waist. Saris come in a wide variety of fabrics, colors, and designs, with different styles and draping techniques specific to different regions of India. The sari is not only a symbol of femininity and grace but also a reflection of India's rich cultural diversity and craftsmanship.

3. **Hanbok (Korea):**

The hanbok is the traditional attire of Korea, characterized by its vibrant colors, flowing lines, and graceful silhouettes. Hanboks are typically made from silk or cotton fabric and consist of a jeogori (jacket) and chima (skirt) for women, and a jeogori and baji (trousers) for men. Hanboks are worn on special occasions such as weddings, New Year celebrations, and traditional holidays, and they are prized for their beauty, craftsmanship, and cultural significance.

4. Dashiki (West Africa):

The dashiki is a colorful, loose-fitting garment worn by men and women in West Africa, particularly in countries such as Nigeria, Ghana, and Senegal. Dashikis are typically made from cotton fabric and feature intricate embroidery and bold patterns that hold symbolic meaning within African culture. Dashikis are often worn as a symbol of African pride and identity, particularly during cultural events, festivals, and ceremonies.

5. Dirndl and Lederhosen (Germany):

The dirndl and lederhosen are traditional garments worn in Bavaria and other regions of Germany, particularly during Oktoberfest and other folk festivals. The dirndl is a dress worn by women, consisting of a bodice, blouse, skirt, and apron, while lederhosen are leather shorts worn by men, often paired with a shirt, vest, and suspenders. Dirndls and lederhosen are symbols of Bavarian heritage and are worn with pride during celebrations of German culture and tradition.

6. Thobe (Middle East):

The thobe, also known as a dishdasha or kandura, is a traditional garment worn by men in many Middle Eastern countries, including Saudi Arabia, Kuwait, and the United Arab Emirates. The thobe is a long, flowing robe made from lightweight fabric, typically white in color, and worn with a headdress such as a ghutra or keffiyeh. The thobe is not only a practical garment for the region's hot climate but also a symbol of modesty, tradition, and cultural identity.

Quirky Customs: Celebrating Unusual Traditions

While many cultural practices and traditions are steeped in centuries of history and tradition, some customs around the world are delightfully quirky, celebrating the unique and unexpected. These offbeat traditions offer a glimpse into the playful and inventive spirit of different cultures and communities, adding color and charm to the tapestry of human experience. From tomato-throwing festivals to underwater pumpkin carving competitions, here are some examples of quirky customs celebrated around the world:

1. La Tomatina (Spain):

La Tomatina is an annual festival held in the town of Buñol, Spain, where participants engage in a massive tomato fight. Held on the last Wednesday of August, the festival attracts thousands of people who gather in the town square to hurl ripe tomatoes at each other for fun. La Tomatina is believed to have originated in the 1940s and has since become one of Spain's most famous and quirky cultural events.

2. Cheese Rolling (United Kingdom):

The Cooper's Hill Cheese-Rolling and Wake is an eccentric annual event held on the Spring Bank Holiday near Gloucester, England. Participants race down a steep hillside in pursuit of a large wheel of cheese, which is rolled down the hill ahead of them. The first person to reach the bottom of the hill and grab the cheese is declared the winner. The event, which dates back to at least the 19th century, attracts participants and spectators from around the world.

3. Boryeong Mud Festival (South Korea):

The Boryeong Mud Festival is an annual event held in the city of Boryeong, South Korea, to promote the region's mineral-rich mud. The festival features a variety of mud-related activities and attractions, including mud baths, mud slides, and mud wrestling competitions. Participants come from all over South Korea and beyond to enjoy the therapeutic properties of the mud and to indulge in some lighthearted fun.

4. Holi Festival (India):

Holi, also known as the Festival of Colors, is a vibrant Hindu festival celebrated in India and other parts of South Asia to mark the arrival of spring and the triumph of good over evil. During Holi, people gather in the streets to throw colored powders and water at each other, creating a kaleidoscope of colors and joy. The festival is also associated with music, dance, and traditional sweets, making it a lively and exuberant celebration.

5. Underwater Pumpkin Carving Contest (United States):

The Underwater Pumpkin Carving Contest is an annual event held in Key Largo, Florida, where scuba divers compete to carve the best pumpkin underwater. Participants dive to the ocean floor with hollowed-out pumpkins and carving tools, where they must contend with the challenges of buoyancy and limited visibility to create their masterpieces. The contest attracts skilled divers and artists from around the world and is a highlight of the Halloween season.

6. Night of the Radishes (Mexico):

The Night of the Radishes, or Noche de Rábanos, is a unique holiday celebrated in the city of Oaxaca, Mexico, on December 23rd. During the event, local artisans carve intricate designs into large radishes, creating elaborate sculptures and dioramas that depict scenes from Mexican folklore, history, and culture. The festival attracts thousands of visitors each year and is a beloved tradition in the region.

Chapter 12
Invisible Worlds: The Microscopic Universe Among Us

The Building Blocks of Life: Cells and Their Functions

Exploring the microscopic universe reveals an intricate world that's foundational to all life forms on Earth. This invisible world is primarily composed of cells, which serve as the basic structural, functional, and biological units of all known living organisms. Here's an overview of cells and their functions, illuminating the complexity and beauty of life at the microscopic level.

Understanding Cells

Cells come in two primary types: Prokaryotic and Eukaryotic.

Prokaryotic Cells: These cells are simpler in structure, lacking a nucleus and most organelles found in more complex cells. Bacteria and archaea are composed of prokaryotic cells. Despite their simplicity, they perform essential functions necessary for their survival, including reproduction, metabolism, and responding to environmental changes.

Eukaryotic Cells: These cells are more complex and are found in plants, animals, fungi, and protists. They have a defined nucleus containing the cell's genetic material and various organelles that perform specific tasks. Eukaryotic cells are larger than prokaryotic cells and have intricate structures that enable them to execute a wide range of functions, including energy production, waste disposal, and reproduction.

Key Organelles and Their Functions

Nucleus: The control center of the cell, containing DNA and responsible for regulating gene expression and cell division.
Mitochondria: Known as the powerhouse of the cell, mitochondria generate ATP, the cell's energy currency, through cellular respiration.
Chloroplasts (in plant cells): Sites of photosynthesis, where sunlight is converted into chemical energy.
Ribosomes: Responsible for protein synthesis, translating genetic information into proteins necessary for cell function.

Endoplasmic Reticulum (ER): Involved in protein and lipid synthesis; the rough ER is studded with ribosomes, while the smooth ER lacks them and is involved in lipid synthesis.
Golgi Apparatus: Modifies, sorts, and packages proteins and lipids for storage or transport out of the cell.
Lysosomes: Contain digestive enzymes to break down macromolecules, old cell parts, and foreign invaders.
Cell Membrane: A lipid bilayer that surrounds the cell, controlling the movement of substances in and out of the cell and enabling communication with other cells.

The Role of Cells in Life

Cells are not just the building blocks of living organisms; they are dynamic entities that interact with their environment in complex ways. They can communicate with each other through chemical signals, respond to external stimuli, and adapt to changing conditions. The study of cells, known as cell biology or cytology, is crucial for understanding diseases, developing medical treatments, and exploring the fundamental processes of life.

The microscopic universe of cells reveals the profound complexity of life, showing that even the smallest entities are equipped with extraordinary capabilities to sustain life, reproduce, and evolve. This invisible world is a testament to the intricate design and interconnectivity of biological systems, highlighting the wonder and resilience of life on Earth.

Viruses and Bacteria: Tiny Entities, Huge Impact

The microscopic universe teems with a myriad of tiny organisms, among which viruses and bacteria stand out for their immense impact on the environment, human health, and the course of history. Despite their minuscule size, these microorganisms play critical roles in our world's ecosystems, including influencing climate patterns, shaping biological evolution, and affecting the health of all living beings.

Viruses: The Borderline of Life

Viruses are incredibly small entities, often around 100 times smaller than most bacteria. They are unique in that they exist on the borderline of what we consider "alive." Viruses cannot reproduce or carry out metabolic processes on their own. Instead, they must infect a host cell and hijack its machinery to replicate. This ability to infect hosts ranges from bacteria (bacteriophages) to plants and animals, causing diseases like the flu, HIV/AIDS, and COVID-19.

Characteristics and Impact

Structure: Viruses consist of genetic material (DNA or RNA) enclosed in a protein coat called a capsid. Some viruses also have an outer lipid envelope.

Diversity: There is an incredible variety of viruses, adapted to infect almost every type of living organism.

Role in Disease: Viruses are responsible for a wide range of diseases in humans, animals, and plants. They can cause mild symptoms, severe illness, or even death.

Biotechnological Applications: Viruses have been used in gene therapy, vaccine development, and as tools in molecular biology.

Bacteria: The Ubiquitous Microorganisms

Bacteria are single-celled prokaryotic organisms that are found in virtually every habitat on Earth, from soil and water to extreme environments such as hot springs and radioactive waste. They come in various shapes, including spheres (cocci), rods (bacilli), and spirals (spirilla).

Functions and Importance

Ecosystem Roles: Bacteria are essential for nutrient cycling, decomposing organic material, and supporting the base of food webs.

Human Health: While some bacteria cause diseases like tuberculosis, pneumonia, and salmonellosis, many others are beneficial and essential for human health. The human microbiome, for example, is composed of trillions of bacteria that aid in digestion, protect against pathogens, and contribute to the immune system's function.

Biotechnology and Industry: Bacteria have numerous applications in industry and biotechnology, including the production of antibiotics, the fermentation of food, and the cleanup of oil spills through bioremediation.

The Dual Nature of Viruses and Bacteria

Both viruses and bacteria can be agents of disease, yet they also play indispensable roles in ecosystems and human health. Their ability to adapt and evolve makes them significant both as threats and as tools for scientific advancement. The study of these microorganisms not only helps in understanding and combating infectious diseases but also in exploring new ways to harness their capabilities for beneficial applications.

Understanding the complex roles of viruses and bacteria underscores the delicate balance between humans and the microscopic world. These tiny entities, though often unseen, continue to have a huge impact on life on Earth, driving home the point that size does not dictate significance in the vast tapestry of life.

The Microbiome: Microorganisms and Their Role in Health

The human microbiome is a complex ecosystem made up of trillions of microorganisms, including bacteria, viruses, fungi, and other microscopic life forms. These microorganisms reside primarily in the gut but are also found on the skin, in the mouth, and in other parts of the body where they interact with their environment and the human host. The study of the microbiome has revolutionized our understanding of health and disease, revealing that these tiny inhabitants play a crucial role in maintaining physiological balance and influencing overall well-being.

Composition and Diversity of the Microbiome
The human microbiome is incredibly diverse, with the gut alone hosting up to 1000 different species of bacteria. The composition of this microbial community varies significantly from one individual to another, influenced by factors such as diet, lifestyle, genetics, and exposure to antibiotics and other drugs.

Key Functions of the Microbiome

Digestion and Nutrition: The gut microbiome assists in breaking down complex carbohydrates and fibers that the human body cannot digest on its own, producing short-chain fatty acids that serve as an energy source for the body and help maintain the health of the gut lining.
Immune System Modulation: Microorganisms in the microbiome play a crucial role in developing and training the immune system. They help distinguish between harmless and harmful pathogens, thus preventing autoimmune diseases.
Protection Against Pathogens: By occupying space and resources, beneficial microorganisms in the microbiome can prevent the colonization and growth of pathogenic bacteria, a phenomenon known as colonization resistance.
Mental Health: Emerging research suggests a connection between the gut microbiome and the brain, often referred to as the "gut-brain axis." This relationship indicates that the state of the gut microbiome can affect mood, cognitive function, and the risk of developing neurological conditions.

The Microbiome and Diseases

Imbalances in the microbiome, known as dysbiosis, have been linked to a wide range of diseases, including obesity, diabetes, inflammatory bowel disease (IBD), allergies, and even mental health disorders such as depression and anxiety. Understanding these connections is crucial for developing new therapeutic strategies that target the microbiome to treat and prevent disease.

Modulating the Microbiome for Better Health

Lifestyle and dietary choices can significantly impact the composition and function of the microbiome. Consuming a diverse diet rich in fiber, reducing antibiotic use, and avoiding excessive hygiene practices can help maintain a healthy and balanced microbiome. Additionally, probiotics (live beneficial bacteria) and prebiotics (fibers that feed these bacteria) are being explored for their potential to support microbiome health.

The World of Fungi: Decomposers and Symbionts

The world of fungi encompasses a vast and diverse kingdom that plays critical roles in Earth's ecosystems. Fungi are neither plants nor animals; they form a distinct kingdom of organisms that include yeasts, molds, and mushrooms. These organisms are essential decomposers and symbionts, breaking down dead organic material and recycling nutrients, as well as forming beneficial associations with plants, animals, and other organisms. The intricate roles fungi play in the environment, along with their unique biological characteristics, underscore their importance in maintaining the balance of life on our planet.

Fungi as Decomposers

One of the primary roles of fungi in ecosystems is as decomposers. They break down dead and decaying organic matter, including leaves, wood, and deceased animals. This decomposition process is vital for nutrient cycling, as it converts complex organic materials into simpler compounds that can be readily used by plants and other organisms.

Wood Decomposition: Fungi are among the few organisms capable of breaking down lignin, a complex polymer in wood that is highly resistant to degradation. This ability allows fungi to play a crucial role in decomposing trees and other woody plants.

Soil Health: By decomposing organic matter, fungi contribute to soil structure and fertility, enhancing its ability to support plant life.

Fungi as Symbionts

Fungi also form symbiotic relationships with plants, animals, and other organisms, benefiting both the fungi and their hosts.

Mycorrhizal Fungi: These fungi form associations with plant roots, increasing the plant's access to water and nutrients such as phosphorus and nitrogen. In exchange, the plant supplies the fungi with carbohydrates produced through photosynthesis. This relationship is critical for the health and productivity of many ecosystems, including forests and agricultural lands.

Lichens: Lichens are complex life forms that arise from the symbiotic relationship between fungi and photosynthetic organisms, such as algae or cyanobacteria. The fungi provide a structure that protects the photosynthetic organisms from environmental conditions, while the latter produce nutrients through photosynthesis to feed the fungi. Lichens are essential for colonizing and stabilizing barren surfaces, such as rocks, and contributing to soil formation.

Economic and Medical Importance

Beyond their environmental roles, fungi have significant economic and medical implications.

Antibiotics: The discovery of penicillin, the first antibiotic, from the fungus Penicillium notatum, revolutionized medicine by providing a means to combat bacterial infections effectively.
Food Production: Many fungi are essential in food production and fermentation processes, including the making of bread, cheese, beer, and wine.
Biotechnology: Fungi are used in biotechnology for the production of enzymes, vitamins, and other biochemicals.

Challenges and Threats
While fungi are integral to ecosystem functions and offer various benefits, they can also pose challenges. Some fungi are pathogenic to plants and animals, including humans, causing diseases that can lead to significant agricultural losses or health problems. Moreover, the rapid environmental changes and habitat destruction pose threats to fungal diversity, impacting the delicate balance of ecosystems.

Microscopic Ecosystems: Life in a Drop of Water

A single drop of water, seemingly insignificant and easily overlooked, is a microcosm teeming with life, showcasing the diversity and complexity of microscopic ecosystems. This miniature world is home to a variety of organisms, including bacteria, protozoa, algae, and microscopic invertebrates. These organisms form a complex food web, playing various roles as producers, consumers, and decomposers, demonstrating the interconnectedness of life on even the smallest scales.

The Inhabitants of a Water Drop

Bacteria: These are among the most basic and widespread organisms in water droplets, performing essential roles in recycling nutrients by breaking down organic matter.

Protozoa: Single-celled eukaryotes that consume bacteria, organic matter, and other protozoa. They include amoebas, which move and feed using pseudopods (false feet), and ciliates, which use hair-like cilia for movement and feeding.

Algae: Microscopic plants that photosynthesize, producing oxygen and serving as a primary food source for other microorganisms in the ecosystem.

Microscopic Invertebrates: These include rotifers, copepods, and water fleas (Daphnia). They feed on algae, bacteria, and protozoa, playing a crucial role in controlling populations and recycling nutrients.

Dynamics of Microscopic Ecosystems

In a drop of water, the balance of life is maintained through the interactions among its inhabitants. Algae and cyanobacteria provide the base of the food web, producing oxygen and organic compounds through photosynthesis. These producers are consumed by various protozoans and microscopic invertebrates, which in turn may be preyed upon by larger microorganisms or small aquatic animals. Bacteria decompose dead organic material, recycling nutrients back into the ecosystem to be used by algae and other producers.

Importance of Microscopic Ecosystems

Biological Indicators: The health and composition of microscopic communities in water can indicate the overall health of the water body and its suitability for larger organisms, including humans.

Nutrient Cycling: Microscopic organisms play a critical role in cycling essential nutrients such as carbon, nitrogen, and phosphorus, contributing to the fertility and productivity of aquatic environments.

Food Web Support: These microorganisms form the foundation of aquatic food webs, supporting the life of larger organisms, from fish to waterfowl and ultimately humans.

Challenges Facing Microscopic Ecosystems

Microscopic ecosystems are not immune to environmental changes. Pollution, climate change, and habitat destruction can alter the delicate balance of these communities, affecting water quality and the broader ecosystem services they provide. The proliferation of harmful algae blooms, driven by nutrient pollution and warming temperatures, is one such challenge that can have dire consequences for aquatic life and human health.

The Fascination of Microscopic Life
Exploring life in a drop of water reveals the incredible diversity and resilience of microscopic organisms. It highlights the importance of even the smallest ecosystems in sustaining life on Earth. Advanced microscopy and molecular techniques continue to unveil the secrets of these tiny worlds, expanding our understanding of biological complexity and the interconnectedness of all life forms. Through the lens of a microscope, a drop of water transforms into a bustling metropolis of life, a reminder of the unseen worlds that thrive beyond our immediate perception.

Chapter 13
The Enigma of Time: Its Passage and Perception

Measuring Time: From Sundials to Atomic Clocks

The measurement of time has been a fundamental aspect of human civilization, evolving from ancient methods to the precise technologies of today. This journey from sundials to atomic clocks illustrates not just advances in technology but also our changing relationship with time itself, marking a fascinating progression in our quest to understand and quantify one of the universe's most enigmatic dimensions.

Ancient Timekeeping

Sundials: Among the earliest timekeeping devices, sundials use the position of the sun's shadow cast by a gnomon (a vertical rod) to indicate the time of day. Sundials were used in ancient civilizations across Egypt, Greece, and Rome, reflecting a deep understanding of the sun's movement.
Water Clocks: Also known as clepsydras, water clocks measured time by the regulated flow of liquid from one container to another. Used in various ancient cultures, including China, India, and Greece, they were among the first attempts to measure time independently of natural phenomena like the sun's motion.

Mechanical Clocks
The invention of mechanical clocks in the 13th century marked a significant leap forward. Powered by weights or springs, these clocks used a series of gears and escapements to regulate motion, enabling more precise timekeeping than was possible with sundials or water clocks. The development of the pendulum clock in the 17th century further improved accuracy.

Quartz Clocks
The next major advancement came with the invention of the quartz clock in the 1920s. Quartz clocks use the piezoelectric properties of quartz crystals, which vibrate at a precise frequency when an electric charge is applied. These vibrations can be measured to keep time with remarkable accuracy, making quartz clocks a standard for everyday use.

Atomic Clocks

The pinnacle of precision timekeeping is the atomic clock, first developed in the 1950s. Atomic clocks measure the vibrations of atoms to keep time. The most common type uses the resonance frequencies of cesium atoms to define the second. Atomic clocks are so precise that they will not lose or gain a second for millions of years.

Functioning: Atomic clocks work by measuring the electromagnetic radiation emitted or absorbed by atoms when they change energy levels. The frequency of this radiation is incredibly stable and consistent, making it an ideal standard for measuring time.
Applications: The accuracy of atomic clocks has profound implications for technology and science. They are essential for the Global Positioning System (GPS), telecommunications, and in the study of the fundamental laws of physics.

The Evolution of Time Standards

The definition of a second has evolved alongside advancements in timekeeping technology. Initially based on Earth's rotation, the second was redefined in 1967 by the International System of Units (SI) as the duration of 9,192,631,770 periods of the radiation corresponding to the transition between two hyperfine levels of the ground state of the cesium-133 atom, a measure made possible by the precision of atomic clocks.

The Perception of Time

As timekeeping technology has advanced, so too has our perception of time. Ancient timekeeping methods reflected a direct relationship with the natural world, while modern atomic timekeeping represents an abstract and scientifically precise understanding of time. This evolution underscores the complexity of time as both a physical phenomenon and a concept deeply intertwined with human consciousness and society's development.

The journey from sundials to atomic clocks encapsulates humanity's enduring quest to comprehend and measure time, reflecting our fascination with understanding the universe and our place within it. As we continue to refine our methods of timekeeping, we delve deeper into the enigma of time, unraveling its mysteries while acknowledging its profound impact on our lives.

Time in the Animal Kingdom: How Creatures Perceive Duration

The perception of time in the animal kingdom is a fascinating area of study that reveals a wide range of experiences and adaptations among different species. Unlike humans, who have developed complex systems and technologies to measure and understand time, animals rely on innate abilities and environmental cues to perceive duration and regulate their behavior. This innate sense of time plays a crucial role in survival, influencing activities such as hunting, foraging, migration, and reproduction.

Circadian Rhythms: The Internal Clock

Most animals possess an internal biological clock, known as a circadian rhythm, which follows roughly a 24-hour cycle. This internal clock helps regulate sleep patterns, feeding behavior, and hormonal changes in response to the cycle of day and night. For example, nocturnal animals become active at night, relying on their circadian rhythm to optimize their behavior for the dark hours.

Seasonal Changes and Time Perception

Many animals have developed the ability to perceive longer time intervals, such as seasonal changes, which influence migration patterns, hibernation, and breeding cycles. Birds, for example, migrate based on a combination of genetic predisposition and environmental cues like temperature and day length, indicating an innate understanding of seasonal timing.

Time Perception in Hunting and Avoiding Predators

The perception of time is critical in the context of hunting and avoiding predators. Animals like cheetahs, which rely on speed, must have an acute sense of timing to catch their prey at the right moment. Similarly, prey animals, such as rabbits, have to time their reactions precisely to evade predators, suggesting a highly developed perception of short intervals of time.

Interval Timing and Memory

Research has shown that some animals are capable of interval timing, which is the ability to measure the duration between two events. This skill is crucial for activities such as foraging, where animals must remember the time elapsed since they last visited a food source. Studies on bees, for instance, have demonstrated their ability to remember the timing of flower nectar availability, optimizing their foraging efficiency.

The Role of the Brain in Time Perception

The neural mechanisms behind time perception in animals are an area of ongoing research. It is believed that the brain's ability to process sensory information and create temporal memories plays a significant role in how animals perceive time. For example, the suprachiasmatic nucleus in mammals is a key component of the circadian system, regulating the body's internal clock in response to light cues.

Unique Time-Sensing Abilities

Some animals display unique time-sensing abilities that are still not fully understood. For instance, dogs have been reported to anticipate the arrival of their owners at consistent times, even without obvious cues. This ability might be linked to a combination of circadian rhythms and associative learning, highlighting the complexity of time perception in the animal world.

The study of time perception in animals offers valuable insights into the evolutionary adaptations that enable survival in a dynamic environment. It underscores the diversity of life on Earth and the sophisticated ways in which living creatures interact with their surroundings. As research progresses, we continue to uncover the intricate mechanisms that govern the sense of time across the animal kingdom, revealing a fascinating aspect of the natural world that mirrors our own experiences with the enigma of time.

The Relativity of Time: Speed and Gravity's Role

The concept of time as a relative and not an absolute entity is one of the most groundbreaking revelations of modern physics. This theory, comprising both special and general relativity, fundamentally changed our understanding of time, space, and the universe. It revealed that the passage of time is influenced by speed and gravity, challenging the notion of a universal clock that ticks at the same rate for everyone, everywhere.

Special Relativity and Time Dilation

Special relativity, introduced in 1905, posits that the laws of physics are the same for all non-accelerating observers and that the speed of light in a vacuum is constant, regardless of the motion of the light source or observer. A fascinating consequence of special relativity is time dilation, which occurs at relativistic speeds — close to the speed of light.

Time Dilation: This phenomenon implies that time passes at a slower rate for an object in motion compared to an object at rest. For example, if one twin were to travel into space at near-light speed and return, they would be younger than the twin who stayed on Earth. This effect has been confirmed through experiments, notably using precise atomic clocks on fast-moving airplanes and satellites.

General Relativity and The Impact of Gravity on Time

General relativity, introduced in 1915, extends the principle of relativity to include gravity, describing it not as a force between masses but as a curvature of spacetime caused by mass and energy. According to general relativity, time itself is affected by gravity.

Gravitational Time Dilation: Time moves slower in stronger gravitational fields. This means that time passes slightly faster on the surface of the Earth, where gravity is weaker, compared to closer to a massive object like a planet or a star. This has been observed through experiments comparing the rate at which time passes for clocks on the surface of the Earth to clocks in orbit, where the gravitational pull is weaker.

Implications and Applications

The relativity of time has profound implications for our understanding of the universe and has practical applications in technology.

GPS Systems: The Global Positioning System (GPS) relies on satellites equipped with atomic clocks. The calculations for GPS signals correct for the effects of both special and general relativity, accounting for the faster passage of time due to both the satellites' speed and their position in a weaker gravitational field compared to the Earth's surface.

Understanding the Universe: The concepts of time dilation and gravitational time dilation are critical for astrophysics, including the study of black holes and the expansion of the universe. Near a black hole, for instance, gravitational time dilation becomes extremely significant, leading to scenarios where time for an observer close to the black hole would seem to almost stand still from the perspective of a distant observer.

The relativity of time challenges our intuitive understanding of time as a constant and universal measure. It illustrates that time's passage is intimately connected with the fabric of spacetime, affected by velocity and the presence of mass and energy. This revolutionary concept not only expands our knowledge of the physical universe but also deepens our philosophical inquiries into the nature of reality, time, and existence.

Time Travel: Theories and Possibilities

Time travel, a captivating concept often explored in science fiction, also holds a place in theoretical physics. While the idea of moving freely through time, as one might move through space, remains within the realm of speculation and imagination, certain principles of physics suggest scenarios where time travel could theoretically be possible, albeit with limitations and profound implications.

Traveling Forward in Time: Special Relativity
The concept of time dilation in theory of special relativity provides a scientifically grounded method for traveling forward in time. As an object's speed approaches the speed of light, time slows down for the object relative to a stationary observer. This effect has been experimentally confirmed with particles in accelerators and atomic clocks on fast-moving aircraft. In theory, if a person were to travel in a spacecraft at a significant fraction of the speed of light on a long journey and then return to Earth, they would find that more time had passed on Earth than for them, effectively traveling into the Earth's future.

Traveling Backward in Time: Wormholes and Curved Spacetime
General relativity also suggests mechanisms by which traveling backward in time might be conceivable, though these ideas venture more into the realm of theoretical speculation without experimental evidence.

Wormholes: Also known as Einstein-Rosen bridges, wormholes are hypothetical passages through spacetime that could create shortcuts for long journeys across the universe. If a wormhole could be stabilized (a significant technical challenge, requiring exotic matter with negative energy), and one end of the wormhole was accelerated to near-light speed and then brought back (utilizing time dilation), it could theoretically allow for travel between the two ends of the wormhole across different times.

Closed Timelike Curves (CTCs): General relativity permits the existence of closed timelike curves, which are paths through spacetime that return to the same point in space and time. These CTCs offer a mathematical model for backward time travel but remain speculative without physical evidence or a clear understanding of how they could be created or interacted with.

Challenges and Paradoxes

Time travel, especially backward in time, introduces several paradoxes and challenges that question the feasibility and consequences of such phenomena.

Grandfather Paradox: This is the classic time travel paradox where a traveler goes back in time and prevents their grandfather from meeting their grandmother, potentially erasing the traveler's existence.
Causality: The fundamental principle that cause precedes effect could be violated by time travel, leading to logical contradictions and unpredictable outcomes in the fabric of reality.

Theoretical Limitations and Quantum Considerations

The energy and conditions required for backward time travel (e.g., stabilizing a wormhole) are beyond our current technological capabilities and may remain so. Quantum mechanics introduces additional complexities, with some interpretations suggesting that quantum effects could prevent time travel paradoxes by splitting timelines or universes, aligning with the many-worlds interpretation of quantum theory.

The Cyclical Nature of Time in Cultures and Histories

The perception of time as cyclical is a concept deeply rooted in various cultures and histories around the world. Unlike the linear concept of time, which views time as a straight path from the past through the present to the future, the cyclical view sees time as recurring in patterns, cycles, and seasons. This perspective reflects in the natural world, religious beliefs, and philosophical thoughts, illustrating a profound understanding of the universe's rhythms and the human life cycle.

Nature's Cycles

Many ancient civilizations based their concept of time on the observable cycles in nature, such as the phases of the moon, the changing seasons, and the patterns of stars and planets. These natural phenomena became the foundations for calendars, agricultural practices, and festivals.

Agricultural Societies: For agricultural societies, understanding the cyclical patterns of seasons was crucial for planting and harvesting crops. Festivals celebrating the solstices and equinoxes marked significant times of the year for these communities.

Religious and Mythological Perspectives

In many religious and mythological traditions, the cyclical nature of time is a central theme, often related to creation, preservation, and destruction cycles.

Hinduism: The concept of cyclical time is integral, with the universe going through vast cycles of creation, preservation, and destruction, known as Yugas. The end of one cycle leads to the beginning of a new one, in an eternal series of cosmic birth and rebirth.

Ancient Egypt: The Egyptians observed the annual flooding of the Nile as a cycle of renewal that brought fertility to the land. This natural cycle was deeply intertwined with their religious beliefs, where deities were believed to govern these natural events.

Mayan Civilization: The Mayans developed a complex calendar system that combined linear and cyclical time, with cycles of various lengths to mark religious and astronomical events.

Philosophical Interpretations

Philosophical views on the cyclical nature of time can also be found across different cultures, reflecting on the repetitive aspects of existence and the human condition.

Stoicism: In ancient Greek and Roman philosophy, Stoicism suggested that the universe periodically destroyed itself in a conflagration only to be reborn again, in a cycle of renewal.

Buddhism: The Buddhist concept of Samsara describes a cycle of birth, death, and rebirth, from which individuals can escape only through enlightenment.

Modern Implications

The cyclical perception of time influences contemporary thinking and living, from the celebration of traditional festivals to the understanding of history as patterns that repeat. This view encourages reflection on the lessons of the past and recognition of the natural world's rhythms, fostering a sense of continuity and connection across generations.

The cyclical nature of time, as seen through the lens of various cultures and historical periods, offers a rich and diverse understanding of how humans have made sense of the world around them. It underscores the interconnectedness of life, the environment, and the cosmos, providing insights into the collective human experience and our place within the universe's ever-turning wheel.

Chapter 14
Rhythms of Nature: The Secrets of Seasonal Changes

The Impact of Seasons on Flora and Fauna

Seasonal changes have profound impacts on flora and fauna, driving the rhythms of nature and influencing the behavior, reproduction, and survival of a wide array of species. As the Earth orbits the sun, the tilt of its axis causes variations in the intensity and duration of sunlight received by different parts of the planet, leading to the succession of seasons. These changes signal a range of adaptations in plants and animals, showcasing the intricate balance and interconnectedness of Earth's ecosystems.

Impact on Flora (Plants)

Growth and Dormancy: Many plants exhibit periods of growth and dormancy that coincide with the changing seasons. In spring, warmer temperatures and increased daylight stimulate growth and flowering. In contrast, many trees shed their leaves in autumn as a preparation for winter dormancy, conserving energy by reducing metabolic activity.
Reproductive Cycles: Seasonal changes are closely tied to the reproductive cycles of plants. The timing of flowering in many species is synchronized with specific seasons to optimize pollination. For example, spring flowers bloom to take advantage of increased pollinator activity, while some plants produce seeds in autumn that require cold stratification during winter to germinate in spring.
Photosynthesis: The rate of photosynthesis in plants can vary with the seasons, influenced by changes in daylight, temperature, and water availability. This affects not only individual plant growth but also the overall productivity of ecosystems.

Impact on Fauna (Animals)

Migration: Seasonal changes are a major driver of migration patterns in animals. Birds, fish, mammals, and even insects undertake long journeys to exploit seasonal resources or find more favorable climates. For example, birds migrate to warmer regions during winter to access food supplies that are not available in their breeding territories.
Hibernation and Torpor: Many animals enter states of reduced metabolic activity to conserve energy during periods when food is scarce, primarily in winter. Bears are well-known for hibernating, but

smaller animals like bats and some rodents enter torpor, a short-term hibernation-like state, to survive cold spells.

Breeding Seasons: The reproductive timing in animals often aligns with seasonal changes to ensure that offspring are born during periods of resource abundance. Many species have well-defined breeding seasons triggered by changes in daylight and temperature, ensuring that young animals have the best chance of survival.

Physical Changes: Animals can undergo physical changes in response to the seasons. This includes growing thicker fur or feathers for insulation against cold weather, changing color to blend into seasonal landscapes for camouflage, and accumulating fat reserves for energy.

Ecosystem Dynamics

The interactions between flora and fauna during seasonal changes are critical for maintaining ecosystem dynamics. Plants provide habitat and food for animals, while animals contribute to plant pollination, seed dispersal, and nutrient cycling. Seasonal phenomena, such as wildfires in some ecosystems, can also play natural roles in habitat renewal and species diversity.

Human Impacts and Climate Change

Human activities and climate change are altering seasonal patterns and the timing of biological events (phenology), potentially disrupting the synchronized relationships between species and their environments. Changes in the timing of flowering, migrations, and animal hibernation patterns can lead to mismatches between species, affecting ecosystem health and biodiversity.

The impact of seasons on flora and fauna illustrates the complex, adaptive strategies life on Earth has developed to thrive in a dynamic environment. Understanding these seasonal rhythms is crucial for conservation efforts, as it helps predict how ecosystems might respond to future changes, ensuring the preservation of biodiversity for generations to come.

The Role of Light in Seasonal Behavior

Light plays a pivotal role in driving seasonal behavior across the natural world, acting as a primary environmental cue for many organisms. The changing patterns of daylight and darkness throughout the year, resulting from the Earth's tilt and its orbit around the sun, significantly influence biological rhythms and activities. This light-dependent seasonal behavior is observed in a wide range of life forms, from the smallest plants to the largest mammals, and is crucial for their survival, reproduction, and overall well-being.

Photoperiodism: The Biological Response to Light and Dark Periods

Photoperiodism is the physiological reaction of organisms to the length of day or night. It is a critical mechanism by which organisms regulate their seasonal activities, ensuring they occur at the most advantageous time of year.

Plants: In flora, photoperiodism influences flowering, leaf growth, and dormancy. Some plants are classified as "long-day" or "short-day" plants, depending on whether they require longer daylight periods to flower or shorter ones, respectively. Others, known as "day-neutral" plants, do not rely on daylight length for flowering.
Animals: In fauna, changing daylight lengths trigger breeding cycles, migration, and hibernation behaviors. For example, as days lengthen in spring, birds are stimulated to begin nesting activities, while shorter days in autumn signal deer to enter rutting behavior.

Melatonin and Circadian Rhythms

Melatonin, a hormone produced in the pineal gland, plays a crucial role in regulating circadian rhythms and photoperiodic responses in both animals and humans. The production of melatonin is influenced by the light-dark cycle, with increased production during darkness and suppression in light. This hormone helps organisms distinguish between day and night, influencing sleep patterns, feeding behaviors, and reproductive activities.

Seasonal Affective Disorder (SAD): In humans, the variation in light exposure across seasons can affect melatonin levels, contributing to conditions such as Seasonal Affective Disorder, where individuals experience depressive symptoms during the shorter days of winter.

Migration and Reproductive Cycles

Many species use the changing light of the seasons as signals for migration and reproduction, timing these critical life events to coincide with optimal environmental conditions.

Migration: Birds, fish, and some mammals use the lengthening or shortening of days as cues to start their migratory journeys, ensuring they arrive at breeding or wintering grounds when resources are abundant.
Reproduction: Seasonal changes in daylight also influence the timing of reproductive cycles in many animals. Increasing day length in spring can trigger hormonal changes that prepare animals for breeding, while decreasing daylight signals a time to conserve resources.

Seasonal Adaptations in Plants
Light influences various seasonal adaptations in plants, including the timing of bud burst, leaf fall, and the transition to and from dormancy. These adaptations are critical for survival and reproduction, as they optimize the plant's lifecycle in alignment with seasonal variations in light availability and environmental conditions.

The Impact of Climate Change on Light-Dependent Seasonal Behaviors
Climate change is altering seasonal patterns and potentially disrupting the light-dependent cues that many organisms rely on. Changes in temperature and weather patterns can lead to mismatches between the biological timing of species and the availability of their food sources or suitable habitat conditions, posing challenges to survival and biodiversity.

The role of light in dictating seasonal behavior underscores the intricate connections between organisms and their environment. It highlights the importance of understanding these relationships, especially as global changes threaten to disrupt these finely tuned biological rhythms. Recognizing the fundamental role of light in the natural world can help inform conservation strategies and mitigate the impacts of environmental change.

Seasons of Fertility: Planting and Harvesting Times

The rhythms of nature, marked by the changing seasons, have long dictated the agricultural practices of societies around the world. The knowledge of when to plant and when to harvest is fundamental for ensuring food security and the efficient management of resources. This cyclical pattern of agricultural activities is deeply intertwined with the Earth's seasonal variations, which influence soil temperature, precipitation rates, and daylight hours, all critical factors for the growth and maturation of crops.

Spring: The Season of Planting

Spring marks a period of renewal and growth. As the days lengthen and temperatures rise, the dormant seeds of winter begin to sprout. This season is often seen as an optimal time for planting many crops due to the moist soil conditions and the upcoming warm months that allow plants to grow before the peak summer heat.

Crops: Common spring plantings include leafy greens, peas, onions, potatoes, and some grains. These crops benefit from the cooler early season temperatures and mature before the intense heat of summer.
Regional Variations: The specific timing and type of crops planted in spring can vary significantly depending on local climate and soil conditions.

Summer: Growth and Early Harvests

Summer provides long daylight hours and warm temperatures, conditions that are ideal for the growth and development of many crops. It's a period of vigilance for farmers, who must ensure their crops receive adequate water and protection from pests and diseases.

Crops: Many fruits and vegetables reach maturity in summer, including tomatoes, corn, cucumbers, and berries. Summer is also crucial for the growth of staple grains like wheat and barley in temperate regions.
Harvesting: Early summer sees the harvesting of spring-planted crops, while late summer begins the harvest of those planted in late spring or early summer.

Autumn: The Main Harvest Season

Autumn is traditionally the busiest season for farmers, marked by the harvesting of summer-planted crops before the onset of winter. The cooler temperatures and diminishing daylight prompt plants to complete their life cycles, making it an ideal time for harvest.

Crops: This season is critical for the harvesting of grains such as rice, maize, and soybeans. Fruits like apples and pears, as well as root vegetables like carrots and potatoes, are also harvested during this time.
Preparation for Winter: Farmers also use this time to prepare the land for winter, including planting cover crops to enrich the soil and prevent erosion.

Winter: Planning and Preparation

In many regions, winter is a time of rest for the land, but not for the farmer. It's a period for planning the next planting season, repairing tools and machinery, and ordering seeds.

Crops: In milder climates or with the aid of greenhouses, some hardy vegetables like kale, Brussels sprouts, and certain root vegetables can be grown and harvested during the winter months.
Soil Preparation: Winter is also an important time for preparing the soil for spring planting, including composting and other soil enrichment practices.

The Impact of Climate Change on Seasonal Farming
Climate change is beginning to alter the traditional rhythms of planting and harvesting, with shifts in temperature and precipitation patterns causing farmers to adapt their practices. Unpredictable weather events, changing seasons, and shifts in water availability all pose challenges to traditional farming calendars and food security.

Understanding the seasons of fertility and their impact on planting and harvesting times highlights the deep connection between agriculture and the natural rhythms of the Earth. As the climate continues to change, the knowledge and adaptability of those who work the land will be crucial in continuing to harness these rhythms for food production.

Seasonal Migrations: The Great Journeys

Seasonal migrations represent one of nature's most spectacular phenomena, where countless species embark on long, perilous journeys in response to the changing seasons. These migrations are driven by the need to access resources, find breeding grounds, or escape harsh weather conditions. They are a testament to the resilience and adaptability of wildlife, showcasing the incredible lengths to which animals will go to survive and reproduce. From the vast wildebeest herds traversing the African savannas to the delicate monarch butterflies traveling thousands of miles, seasonal migrations highlight the interconnectedness of Earth's ecosystems.

Wildebeest Migration in the Serengeti
One of the most awe-inspiring migrations is the annual journey of over 1.5 million wildebeest, along with hundreds of thousands of zebras and gazelles, across the Serengeti ecosystem in Tanzania and into the Maasai Mara in Kenya. This migration is driven by the search for fresh grazing grounds and water, following the seasonal rains. The perilous journey is fraught with dangers, including predators and treacherous river crossings, yet it is crucial for the survival of these species.

Arctic Terns: The Longest Migration
The Arctic tern holds the record for the longest migration of any animal in the world. These small birds travel an astonishing 71,000 kilometers (about 44,000 miles) annually from their Arctic breeding grounds to the Antarctic coast and back again. This round trip ensures they experience two summers per year, taking advantage of the endless daylight to feed and breed.

Monarch Butterfly Migration
The migration of the monarch butterfly is another remarkable journey, spanning up to 4,000 miles. Each fall, millions of monarchs fly from their summer breeding grounds in the northeastern United States and Canada to their wintering sites in the mountainous oyamel fir forests of Central Mexico. This migration is unique because it spans multiple

generations; the butterflies that return north in the spring are the great-grandchildren of those that migrated south the previous fall.

Humpback Whale Migration

Humpback whales undertake extensive migrations from their feeding grounds in polar waters to warmer tropical and subtropical waters to breed and give birth. These journeys can span thousands of miles and are essential for the survival of their calves, which are born without the thick blubber needed to survive in cold waters.

Salmon Runs

Salmon are famous for their dramatic upstream migrations to the freshwater streams where they were born. After spending several years in the ocean, they return to their natal rivers to spawn, often leaping up waterfalls and navigating obstacles. After spawning, most salmon die, and their bodies provide important nutrients to the river ecosystems.

The Impact of Climate Change on Migrations

Climate change poses significant challenges to migratory species, altering habitats, shifting the timing of food availability, and changing temperature and weather patterns. These disruptions can lead to mismatches between migratory species and the resources they depend on, threatening their survival.

Seasonal migrations are a powerful reminder of the natural world's rhythms and the extraordinary lengths to which species will go to ensure their continuity. They underscore the importance of conserving migratory routes and habitats, not just for the migratory species themselves but for the health of global ecosystems. As we witness these great journeys, we are reminded of the resilience of life and the need to protect the delicate balance that sustains it.

Hibernation and Dormancy: Survival Strategies

Hibernation and dormancy are remarkable survival strategies employed by various species to overcome the challenges posed by seasonal changes, particularly during cold or arid periods when food resources become scarce. These adaptations allow organisms to conserve energy, reduce metabolic needs, and survive adverse conditions until more favorable times return.

Hibernation in Animals

Hibernation is a state of deep sleep or torpor that allows animals to survive winter months when food is scarce and temperatures are low. During hibernation, an animal's metabolic rate significantly decreases, reducing its need for food and enabling it to live off stored body fat.

Bears: Often cited as the classic example of hibernators, bears enter a state of hibernation that can last for months. While their body temperature only drops slightly, their metabolic rate decreases dramatically, allowing them to go without eating, drinking, urinating, or defecating for the duration of their hibernation.
Small Mammals: Rodents like ground squirrels and hamsters exhibit a more profound form of hibernation, with body temperatures dropping close to the ambient temperature and metabolic rates decreasing to just 2-5% of normal levels.
Amphibians and Reptiles: Some amphibians and reptiles also undergo a form of hibernation known as brumation. Unlike mammalian hibernation, these cold-blooded animals experience a period of dormancy that involves very little movement but does not involve the same degree of metabolic slowdown.

Dormancy in Plants

Dormancy in plants is a survival strategy to cope with unfavorable environmental conditions, such as winter cold or summer drought. During dormancy, growth and metabolic processes slow down, and plants may shed their leaves to minimize water loss and reduce energy expenditure.

Deciduous Trees: In temperate regions, deciduous trees lose their leaves in autumn as a way to reduce water loss through transpiration and to conserve energy during the cold winter months.
Perennials: Many perennial plants retreat to their roots, where they store energy in the form of carbohydrates to survive the winter. In spring, these reserves fuel the plant's reemergence.

Seeds: Many plants produce seeds that enter a dormant state until conditions are favorable for germination, ensuring the species' survival across varying environmental conditions.

The Role of Environmental Cues

Both hibernation and dormancy are triggered by environmental cues such as temperature changes, decreased food availability, and changes in daylight hours. These cues signal the approaching unfavorable conditions, prompting organisms to prepare by accumulating energy reserves or altering physiological processes.

Climate Change Impacts

The timing and duration of hibernation and dormancy are finely tuned to specific environmental cues, which are becoming increasingly unpredictable due to climate change. Warmer temperatures and altered precipitation patterns can disrupt the natural cycles of hibernation and dormancy, potentially leading to mismatches between an organism's physiological state and the availability of resources.

Hibernation and dormancy illustrate the complex and dynamic interactions between organisms and their environments. These strategies are crucial for the survival of many species, allowing them to navigate the challenges of seasonal changes. Understanding these processes not only highlights the resilience and adaptability of life but also underscores the importance of maintaining the natural rhythms and balances within ecosystems in the face of global environmental changes.

Chapter 15
Unexplored and Remote Places

The Least Populated Places on Earth

While much of the world's population is concentrated in urban centers and densely populated regions, there are remote and sparsely inhabited areas where few people reside. These least populated places often boast stunning natural landscapes, pristine environments, and unique cultures. Here are some of the least populated places on Earth:

1. Antarctica:

As the southernmost continent, Antarctica is the coldest, driest, and windiest place on Earth. It is also one of the least populated places, with no permanent residents. While scientific research stations are present, they are inhabited only by rotating teams of researchers and support staff. The population fluctuates depending on the season, with more people during the austral summer and fewer during the harsh winter months.

2. Greenland:

Greenland, an autonomous territory within the Kingdom of Denmark, is the world's largest island and the least densely populated territory in the world. Despite its vast size, Greenland has a population of only around 56,000 people, primarily concentrated along the coast. Much of the interior of the island is uninhabited due to its harsh Arctic climate and rugged terrain.

3. Pitcairn Islands:

The Pitcairn Islands, a British Overseas Territory in the South Pacific Ocean, consist of four volcanic islands: Pitcairn, Henderson, Ducie, and Oeno. Pitcairn Island is the only inhabited island, with a population of around 50 people, mostly descendants of the Bounty mutineers and their Tahitian companions. The remote location and limited accessibility contribute to its small population.

4. Svalbard, Norway:

Svalbard is a remote archipelago located in the Arctic Ocean, midway between mainland Norway and the North Pole. Despite its expansive territory, Svalbard has a sparse population of around 2,600 people, mainly concentrated in the administrative center of Longyearbyen. The harsh Arctic climate and limited economic opportunities deter large-scale human settlement.

5. Falkland Islands:
The Falkland Islands, a British Overseas Territory in the South Atlantic Ocean, are sparsely populated, with a population of approximately 3,400 people. Most of the population resides in the capital, Stanley, while the rest are scattered across the islands' rural settlements. The Falkland Islands' remote location and rugged terrain contribute to its low population density.

6. Yukon Territory, Canada:
The Yukon Territory in northern Canada is known for its vast wilderness, rugged mountains, and pristine landscapes. Despite its expansive territory, the Yukon has a population of only around 40,000 people, making it one of the least populated regions in Canada. Much of the territory is uninhabited wilderness, with small communities scattered across the remote landscape.

Remote Islands and Inaccessible Locations

Islands and remote locations often capture the imagination with their isolation, unique ecosystems, and untouched beauty. From uninhabited atolls to rugged landscapes accessible only by intrepid adventurers, these places hold a special allure for explorers and travelers seeking solitude and natural wonders. Here are some examples of remote islands and inaccessible locations around the world:

1. Tristan da Cunha:
Tristan da Cunha is one of the most remote inhabited islands in the world, located in the South Atlantic Ocean. It is part of the British Overseas Territory of Saint Helena, Ascension, and Tristan da Cunha. Home to around 250 residents, the island is known for its isolation, with the nearest inhabited landmass, Saint Helena, located over 2,000 kilometers away.

2. Bouvet Island:

Bouvet Island is an uninhabited volcanic island in the South Atlantic Ocean, making it one of the most remote places on Earth. It is a territory of Norway and is located approximately halfway between Antarctica and the southern tip of Africa. Due to its harsh climate, rugged terrain, and icy surroundings, Bouvet Island is rarely visited by humans.

3. Pitcairn Islands:

The Pitcairn Islands, a group of four volcanic islands in the South Pacific Ocean, are some of the most isolated inhabited islands in the world. Pitcairn Island is the only inhabited island, with a population of around 50 people, primarily descendants of the HMS Bounty mutineers. The islands are a British Overseas Territory known for their remote location and pristine environment.

4. Easter Island:

Easter Island, or Rapa Nui, is a remote island in the southeastern Pacific Ocean, known for its iconic moai statues. Part of Chile, Easter Island is located over 3,500 kilometers from the nearest inhabited landmass. Its isolation and enigmatic stone sculptures make it a fascinating destination for travelers.

5. Svalbard, Norway:

Svalbard is a remote archipelago in the Arctic Ocean, situated midway between mainland Norway and the North Pole. It is known for its rugged landscapes, polar bears, and unique wildlife. Despite its harsh climate, Svalbard is home to several research stations and small settlements, including the administrative center of Longyearbyen.

6. Mount Everest:

Mount Everest, the world's highest peak, located in the Himalayas on the border between Nepal and China (Tibet), is one of the most inaccessible locations on Earth. Climbing Everest presents numerous challenges, including extreme altitudes, harsh weather conditions, and treacherous terrain. Despite these obstacles, it remains a coveted destination for mountaineers seeking to conquer the world's tallest mountain.

The Mystery of Uncontacted Tribes

Uncontacted tribes, also known as isolated or uncontacted peoples, are indigenous groups that have had little to no contact with the outside world and maintain a traditional way of life largely untouched by modern civilization. These tribes inhabit some of the most remote and inaccessible regions of the world, living in harmony with their natural surroundings and maintaining cultural practices passed down through generations. The existence of uncontacted tribes raises questions about human diversity, the impact of globalization, and the importance of preserving indigenous cultures. Here are some key aspects of the mystery surrounding uncontacted tribes:

1. Locations:
Uncontacted tribes are typically found in remote and isolated regions of tropical rainforests, dense jungles, remote islands, and mountainous areas. These areas often provide a natural barrier to outsiders and have limited accessibility, allowing uncontacted tribes to remain hidden from the outside world.

2. Limited Contact:
Uncontacted tribes have deliberately chosen to remain isolated from mainstream society, often due to past experiences of violence, exploitation, or disease introduced by outsiders. As a result, they avoid contact with outsiders and may react defensively to perceived threats or intrusions into their territory.

3. Cultural Practices:
Uncontacted tribes maintain traditional cultural practices, including hunting, gathering, fishing, and subsistence agriculture. They have developed intricate knowledge of their local ecosystems, medicinal plants, and survival skills, enabling them to thrive in their natural environment.

4. Protection and Preservation:
Uncontacted tribes are among the most vulnerable populations in the world, facing threats from deforestation, resource extraction, land encroachment, and diseases introduced by outsiders. Efforts to protect and preserve uncontacted tribes often involve establishing protected

areas, implementing policies to restrict access to their territories, and promoting awareness of their rights and cultural significance.

5. Ethical Considerations:

The ethical dilemma surrounding uncontacted tribes revolves around the principles of self-determination, cultural autonomy, and the right to choose their own way of life. While some argue for non-interference and respect for their isolation, others advocate for intervention to address potential threats to their well-being and human rights.

6. Challenges of Study:

Studying uncontacted tribes presents numerous challenges, including ethical concerns, logistical difficulties, and the risk of inadvertently causing harm or disruption to their communities. Ethical guidelines and protocols have been established to ensure that any contact or engagement with uncontacted tribes is conducted with the utmost sensitivity and respect for their autonomy.

Inhospitable Terrains: Deserts, Tundras, and Jungles

The world's inhospitable terrains encompass a variety of extreme environments, from scorching deserts to frozen tundras and dense jungles. These landscapes present formidable challenges to human survival, yet they are also home to unique ecosystems and diverse wildlife. Exploring these inhospitable terrains offers insights into the resilience of life and the intricate balance of nature. Here's a closer look at deserts, tundras, and jungles:

1. Deserts:

Deserts are arid regions characterized by sparse vegetation, low precipitation, and extreme temperature fluctuations. Despite their harsh conditions, deserts support a surprising array of life adapted to survive in arid environments. Examples of notable deserts include:

- **Sahara Desert:** The Sahara is the world's largest hot desert, covering much of North Africa. It spans several countries, including Morocco, Algeria, Egypt, and Sudan, and features vast sand dunes, rocky plateaus, and oases inhabited by diverse flora and fauna.

- **Atacama Desert:** Located in South America, the Atacama Desert is one of the driest places on Earth. Its barren landscapes, salt flats, and towering volcanoes are home to specialized organisms adapted to extreme aridity, including cacti, lichens, and unique microorganisms.

2. Tundras:

Tundras are treeless, cold biomes found in high-latitude regions near the Arctic and Antarctic Circles. They are characterized by permafrost, low-growing vegetation, and harsh winters. Despite their harsh climate, tundras support a variety of wildlife adapted to cold temperatures. Examples of notable tundras include:

- **Arctic Tundra:** The Arctic tundra spans the northern regions of North America, Europe, and Asia. It is home to iconic species such as polar bears, Arctic foxes, caribou, and musk oxen, as well as migratory birds that breed in the summer months.

- **Antarctic Tundra:** The Antarctic tundra encompasses the continent of Antarctica and its surrounding islands. It is the coldest, driest, and windiest place on Earth, with temperatures plunging well below freezing. Despite its extreme conditions, Antarctic tundra supports diverse marine life, including penguins, seals, and whales.

3. Jungles:

Jungles are dense, tropical forests characterized by lush vegetation, high humidity, and abundant rainfall. They are among the most biodiverse ecosystems on Earth, teeming with a variety of plant and animal species. Examples of notable jungles include:

- **Amazon Rainforest:** The Amazon Rainforest is the largest tropical rainforest in the world, spanning nine countries in South America. It is home to an estimated 10% of the world's known species, including jaguars, sloths, macaws, and countless plant species.

- **Congo Basin:** The Congo Basin, located in Central Africa, is one of the world's largest tropical rainforests. It is known for its dense canopy, diverse wildlife, and critical role in regulating the global climate. The region is home to endangered species such as gorillas, chimpanzees, and forest elephants.

The Last Great Wilderness Areas

In an increasingly interconnected world, true wilderness areas are becoming rare. These are places where human impact is minimal, ecosystems are relatively intact, and biodiversity thrives. They offer a glimpse into what much of the planet looked like before human civilization transformed it. Here are some of the last great wilderness areas on Earth:

1. Antarctica:

Antarctica is the coldest, driest, windiest, and least inhabited continent on Earth. Its vast ice sheets, glaciers, and remote landscapes make it one of the last true wilderness areas. Protected by the Antarctic Treaty System, which designates the continent as a scientific preserve, Antarctica remains largely untouched by human development.

2. Amazon Rainforest:

The Amazon Rainforest, often referred to as the "lungs of the Earth," is the largest tropical rainforest on the planet. Spanning nine countries in South America, it is home to an astonishing array of plant and animal species, many of which are found nowhere else on Earth. Despite facing threats from deforestation and human encroachment, vast stretches of the Amazon still remain untouched and teeming with life.

3. Greenland Ice Sheet:

Greenland is home to the second-largest ice sheet in the world after Antarctica. Covering about 80% of the island's surface, the Greenland Ice Sheet is a pristine wilderness area of ice, snow, and glaciers. It is relatively untouched by human development and provides critical habitat for Arctic wildlife such as polar bears, Arctic foxes, and seals.

4. Sahara Desert:

The Sahara Desert, the largest hot desert in the world, spans much of North Africa. Despite its harsh conditions, the Sahara contains vast expanses of wilderness where human presence is minimal. These remote areas are home to unique desert-adapted plants and animals, including camels, desert foxes, and rare species of reptiles and insects.

5. Canadian Arctic Archipelago:

The Canadian Arctic Archipelago, comprising thousands of islands in Canada's Arctic region, is one of the last great wilderness areas in North America. Its remote landscapes of ice, tundra, and rugged mountains are home to iconic Arctic species such as polar bears, muskoxen, and Arctic wolves.

6. Papua New Guinea Highlands:

The rugged and mountainous terrain of the Papua New Guinea Highlands is one of the most biologically diverse regions on Earth. Its remote valleys and dense rainforests are home to numerous species of birds, mammals, and plants found nowhere else on the planet. Many indigenous communities in the Highlands maintain traditional ways of life and have limited contact with the outside world.

Chapter 16
Stellar Nursery: The Birth of Stars and Planets

The Formation of Stars: From Dust to Dazzling Light

The formation of stars is a magnificent process that unfolds within the vast, cold expanse of interstellar space. This cosmic journey from dust to dazzling light begins in nebulae, the great clouds of gas and dust scattered throughout galaxies. These stellar nurseries harbor the raw materials for star formation, setting the stage for one of the universe's most awe-inspiring transformations.

The Initial Conditions: Molecular Clouds

Star formation starts in molecular clouds, also known as giant molecular clouds (GMCs). These clouds are predominantly composed of hydrogen gas, with traces of helium and other elements, along with dust. They are cold, dense regions of space, with temperatures near absolute zero, allowing molecules to form and clump together. The most famous molecular cloud, the Orion Nebula, is a prime example of a stellar nursery visible to the naked eye.

The Trigger for Star Formation

Star formation begins when part of a molecular cloud becomes unstable and starts to collapse under its own gravity. This can be triggered by various events, such as shock waves from nearby supernovae, collisions between clouds, or gravitational interactions with other astronomical objects. As the cloud collapses, its density increases, and it breaks into smaller, denser fragments.

The Protostar Stage

As a cloud fragment continues to collapse, its core heats up due to gravitational compression. When the core's temperature reaches about 10,000 Kelvin, it becomes a protostar. This phase is characterized by the protostar accumulating mass from its surrounding envelope of gas and dust. Although it glows due to the heat generated by gravitational contraction, nuclear fusion—the process that powers stars—has not yet begun.

The Birth of a Star: Ignition of Nuclear Fusion

A star is born when the core of the protostar becomes hot and dense enough to initiate nuclear fusion. For most stars, including the Sun, this involves the fusion of hydrogen atoms to form helium, releasing vast amounts of energy in the process. This energy production halts the gravitational collapse, creating a delicate balance between the inward pull of gravity and the outward pressure of nuclear fusion. The onset of nuclear fusion marks the transition from a protostar to a main-sequence star.

The Main Sequence and Beyond

Once a star reaches the main sequence phase, it will spend the majority of its life fusing hydrogen into helium in its core. The length of this phase depends on the star's mass; massive stars burn through their hydrogen quickly and live relatively short lives, while smaller stars like the Sun have lifespans spanning billions of years.

The Role of Dust and Planetary Formation

The dust that is not incorporated into the star plays a crucial role in the formation of planets, moons, and other celestial bodies. Around the new star, a rotating disk of gas and dust—the protoplanetary disk—forms. Over time, dust particles within the disk collide and stick together, gradually building up into planetesimals and, eventually, planets.

The formation of stars is a process that underscores the dynamic and ever-changing nature of the universe. From the collapse of cold, dark clouds to the ignition of nuclear fusion that lights up the cosmos, the birth of a star is a testament to the complex processes that drive cosmic evolution. This cycle of star birth and death, with elements formed in the hearts of stars and scattered across the cosmos, contributes to the rich tapestry of the universe and the very possibility of life itself.

Planetary Systems: The Birth of Worlds

The birth of planets and the formation of planetary systems are intricate processes that unfold within the swirling disks of gas and dust surrounding new stars. These protoplanetary disks, remnants of the star formation process, serve as the fertile grounds from which planets emerge, painting a picture of cosmic creativity and complexity.

The Protoplanetary Disk

After a star forms and begins its life on the main sequence, the material remaining in the surrounding disk starts the process of planetary formation. This disk, composed of gas, dust, and debris, is the foundation upon which planets are built. The distribution of material within the disk is influenced by the newly formed star's gravity, radiation, and stellar winds, setting the stage for the birth of worlds.

The Process of Accretion

Planetary formation begins with the process of accretion, where dust particles in the disk collide and stick together, forming larger and larger bodies. These initial collisions create tiny, solid seedlings that gradually grow into planetesimals, asteroid-like objects several kilometers in diameter.

Terrestrial Planets: Closer to the star, where temperatures are higher, metals and silicates condense to form rocky materials. The accretion of these materials leads to the formation of terrestrial planets, like Earth and Mars.

Gas Giants and Ice Giants: Further from the star, where it's colder, ices can also condense, contributing to the formation of larger cores capable of accumulating substantial amounts of gas. This process leads to the formation of gas giants, like Jupiter and Saturn, and ice giants, like Uranus and Neptune.

The Clearing of the Disk

As planets form, they interact with the disk material, carving out gaps and eventually clearing the area around their orbits. The gravitational influence of these nascent planets can cause them to migrate from their original positions, affecting the architecture of the emerging planetary system. Solar winds from the young star also play a crucial role in dispersing the remaining gas and dust, leaving behind a relatively clear system with planets, moons, asteroids, and comets in orbit.

The Role of Resonances and Instabilities

The dynamics within a young planetary system can be complex, with resonances and gravitational interactions between planets causing significant changes in their orbits. These interactions can lead to the ejection of bodies from the system, collisions between objects, or the stabilization of orbits in resonant configurations. The final arrangement of planets within the system is the result of these complex and often chaotic processes.

Planetary Systems Beyond Our Own
The study of extrasolar planets, or exoplanets, has revealed a stunning diversity of planetary systems in our galaxy. Many of these systems have configurations quite different from our own Solar System, with giant planets close to their stars or highly eccentric orbits. These discoveries have expanded our understanding of planetary system formation and the conditions that might lead to the emergence of habitable worlds.

The Importance of Planetary Systems
The formation of planetary systems is a fundamental process in the cosmos, leading to the creation of diverse worlds and potentially habitable environments. These systems are the cosmic arenas in which the drama of celestial mechanics unfolds, and they hold the keys to understanding the conditions necessary for life as we know it. As we continue to explore our own Solar System and beyond, we delve deeper into the mysteries of planetary formation, seeking to uncover the secrets of how worlds are born and evolve in the vast expanse of the universe.

The Lifecycle of Stars: From Nebulae to Supernovae

The lifecycle of a star is a captivating journey that spans millions to billions of years, encompassing a variety of stages from its birth in a nebula to its eventual demise, which can lead to spectacular phenomena such as supernovae. This lifecycle is not only a testament to the dynamic processes governing the universe but also plays a crucial role in the distribution of elements essential for life as we know it.

Birth in a Nebula

A star's life begins in a molecular cloud or nebula, where regions of higher density within the cloud begin to collapse under their own gravity, forming a protostar. This stage is characterized by the accumulation of gas and dust, with the protostar gradually heating up due to gravitational compression.

Main Sequence: The Star's Prime

Once the core temperature of the protostar reaches a point where hydrogen fusion into helium can occur, the star enters the main sequence phase. This is the longest and most stable period in a star's life, during which it generates energy through nuclear fusion at its core. The size and mass of the star determine its position on the Hertzsprung-Russell diagram, which shows the relationship between a star's brightness and its temperature or color.

Low-Mass Stars: These stars, including our Sun, spend billions of years in the main sequence, gradually using up their hydrogen fuel.
High-Mass Stars: More massive stars burn through their hydrogen much more quickly, leading to shorter main sequence lifespans.

Giant Phases: Expansion and Change

As a star exhausts the hydrogen in its core, it begins to fuse helium into heavier elements, causing the core to contract and the outer layers to expand. This expansion marks the star's evolution into a giant or supergiant, significantly increasing its luminosity.

Red Giants: Low- to intermediate-mass stars, like the Sun, will expand into red giants, eventually shedding their outer layers to form planetary nebulae and leaving behind a white dwarf.

Supergiants: Massive stars become supergiants, continuing to fuse elements in their cores up to iron, after which fusion becomes energetically unfavorable.

The Final Stages

The ultimate fate of a star depends on its mass:

White Dwarfs: The remnants of low- to intermediate-mass stars, white dwarfs are incredibly dense objects that slowly cool and fade over time.

Supernovae and Neutron Stars: If a star is sufficiently massive, it will undergo a catastrophic collapse of its core once iron fusion ends, leading to a supernova explosion. This explosion can leave behind a neutron star, an incredibly dense object composed mostly of neutrons. **Black Holes:** The most massive stars may collapse into black holes, regions of space with gravitational fields so strong that not even light can escape.

Legacy of a Star: Element Formation and Distribution
The process of stellar evolution and death is crucial for the synthesis and distribution of heavier elements throughout the universe. Elements formed in the cores of stars and in the explosive environments of supernovae are scattered across space, contributing to the gas and dust in nebulae from which new stars, planets, and eventually life can arise.

The lifecycle of a star, from its origins in a nebula to its final stages, illustrates the cyclical nature of matter in the universe. It highlights the profound connections between the cosmos and the atoms that make up our bodies, reminding us that we are indeed made of "star stuff."

Exoplanets: Searching for Other Earths

The search for exoplanets, planets outside our solar system, has become one of the most exciting and rapidly evolving areas of astronomy. This quest to find other worlds, especially those that might resemble Earth, aims to answer some of humanity's oldest questions: Are we alone in the universe? Is there another planet out there capable of supporting life?

The Discovery of Exoplanets
The first confirmed discovery of an exoplanet orbiting a Sun-like star was made in 1995, when astronomers Michel Mayor and Didier Queloz detected 51 Pegasi b, a giant planet in a close orbit around its star.

Since then, thousands of exoplanets have been discovered, thanks to advancements in telescopic technology and detection methods.

Methods of Detection

Transit Method: This is the most prolific technique for finding exoplanets. It involves monitoring the light from a star and looking for slight dips in brightness, which occur when a planet passes in front of the star and blocks some of its light.

Radial Velocity Method: This technique measures changes in a star's position due to gravitational tugs from an orbiting planet. It detects shifts in the star's spectral lines, indicating movement toward or away from Earth.

Direct Imaging: Although challenging, direct imaging involves taking pictures of exoplanets by blocking out the light from their host stars. This method has been more successful for planets that are far from their stars and very young, hence hotter and more luminous.

Gravitational Microlensing: This method relies on the gravitational lens effect, where the gravitational field of a star (and its planet) bends the light of a background star, magnifying it and revealing the presence of the planet.

The Search for Earth-like Planets

A significant focus of exoplanet research is the discovery of Earth-sized planets in the habitable zone of their stars—the range of distances where conditions might be right for liquid water to exist on a planet's surface. Planets in this "Goldilocks zone" are considered the most likely to be habitable.

Notable Discoveries

Kepler-186f: Discovered in 2014 by the Kepler Space Telescope, this planet is notable for being the first Earth-sized planet found in the habitable zone of its star.

TRAPPIST-1 System: This system, discovered in 2017, contains seven Earth-sized planets, three of which are in the habitable zone. Its proximity and the number of potentially habitable planets make it one of the most intriguing targets for future study.

Proxima Centauri b: Orbiting the closest star to the Sun, this Earth-sized planet is in the habitable zone, offering a tantalizing target for observations to assess its atmosphere and potential for life.

The Role of Gravity in Shaping the Cosmos

Gravity, the weakest yet most pervasive of the fundamental forces in the universe, plays a monumental role in shaping the cosmos. From the formation of stars and planets to the evolution of galaxies and the overall structure of the universe, gravity's influence is both subtle and profound, acting as the cosmic architect that molds matter and energy over vast scales of space and time.

Gravity in Star and Planet Formation

The process of star and planet formation begins within the dense regions of molecular clouds, where gravity pulls together gas and dust, causing these regions to collapse under their own weight. As a cloud collapses, it breaks into fragments, each potentially forming a new star surrounded by a protoplanetary disk. Within these disks, gravity continues its work, pulling together dust and gas to form planets, moons, asteroids, and comets.

Protostar Formation: The collapse of a cloud fragment under gravity increases the pressure and temperature at the core, eventually leading to the ignition of nuclear fusion and the birth of a new star.
Planetary Accretion: Within the protoplanetary disk, gravity causes particles to coalesce into larger bodies, eventually forming planets and other celestial objects.

The Formation and Evolution of Galaxies

Galaxies, vast islands of stars, gas, and dark matter, owe their existence and diversity to gravity. In the early universe, slight overdensities in the distribution of matter—amplified by gravity—grew over time, leading to the formation of galaxies. Gravity pulls stars and gas into galaxies, and it is responsible for the complex interactions between galaxies, including collisions and mergers that can reshape their structures and trigger new rounds of star formation.

Dark Matter: The behavior of galaxies and their clusters suggests the presence of dark matter, an unseen form of matter that does not emit, absorb, or reflect light but exerts gravitational forces. Dark matter is thought to make up the bulk of the matter in the universe, and its gravitational influence is crucial in holding galaxies together and explaining their rotational speeds.

The Structure of the Universe
On the largest scales, gravity has shaped the very structure of the universe. The distribution of galaxies is not random but forms a vast cosmic web of filaments and voids. Regions of higher density attract more matter through gravity, growing into clusters and superclusters of galaxies, while less dense regions become cosmic voids.

Gravity and Cosmic Evolution
Gravity also drives the lifecycle of stars. For most of a star's life, the inward pull of gravity is balanced by the outward pressure of nuclear fusion in its core. However, when a star exhausts its nuclear fuel, gravity can cause it to collapse, leading to the formation of a white dwarf, neutron star, or black hole, depending on the mass of the original star.

Gravitational Waves
Einstein's theory of general relativity predicted that accelerating masses would produce ripples in spacetime, known as gravitational waves. These waves, first directly detected in 2015, provide a new way of observing and understanding the universe, offering insights into phenomena like merging black holes and neutron stars.

Gravity's role in shaping the cosmos is both foundational and ongoing. It is the force that has organized matter into stars, galaxies, and larger structures since the universe's inception. As our understanding of gravity and its interplay with other forces and dark matter deepens, we continue to unlock the secrets of the cosmos, revealing the underlying structure and dynamics of the universe.

Chapter 17
Global
Environmental
Challenges

Climate Change and Its Impact on the World

Climate change is one of the most pressing global environmental challenges facing the world today. It refers to long-term shifts in temperature, precipitation patterns, sea levels, and other indicators of Earth's climate system, primarily driven by human activities such as burning fossil fuels, deforestation, and industrial processes. The impacts of climate change are wide-ranging and profound, affecting ecosystems, communities, economies, and cultures around the world. Here are some key aspects of climate change and its impact on the world:

1. **Rising Temperatures:** One of the most evident effects of climate change is the overall rise in global temperatures. Over the past century, the Earth's average temperature has increased significantly, leading to more frequent and intense heatwaves, prolonged droughts, and changing weather patterns.

2. **Melting Ice and Rising Sea Levels:** As temperatures rise, glaciers and polar ice caps are melting at an accelerated rate. This contributes to rising sea levels, threatening coastal communities and low-lying areas with inundation, erosion, and saltwater intrusion. Small island nations and vulnerable coastal regions are particularly at risk of displacement and loss of livelihoods.

3. **Extreme Weather Events:** Climate change is linked to an increase in extreme weather events such as hurricanes, cyclones, floods, and wildfires. These events can cause widespread devastation, resulting in loss of life, property damage, displacement, and disruption of essential services.

4. **Impacts on Ecosystems and Biodiversity:** Climate change disrupts ecosystems and biodiversity, affecting species distribution, habitats, and migration patterns. Many plant and animal species are facing extinction as their habitats become unsuitable or disappear altogether due to temperature changes, habitat loss, and altered rainfall patterns.

5. **Food Security and Agriculture:** Changes in temperature and precipitation patterns affect agricultural productivity and food

security. Shifts in growing seasons, increased pest and disease pressure, and water scarcity threaten crop yields and livelihoods, particularly in developing countries where agriculture is a primary source of income and food.

6. **Health Impacts:** Climate change has significant implications for human health, exacerbating risks of heat-related illnesses, respiratory problems from air pollution, waterborne diseases, and vector-borne diseases such as malaria and dengue fever. Vulnerable populations, including children, the elderly, and those living in poverty, are disproportionately affected.

7. **Social and Economic Disparities:** Climate change exacerbates existing social and economic disparities, disproportionately affecting marginalized communities, indigenous peoples, and low-income populations. These communities often have limited resources and resilience to cope with the impacts of climate change, leading to increased vulnerability and inequality.

8. **Global Migration and Conflict:** Climate change-induced environmental degradation, resource scarcity, and extreme weather events can contribute to population displacement, migration, and conflicts over land, water, and natural resources. This can lead to social unrest, political instability, and humanitarian crises, with far-reaching implications for regional and global security.

Conservation Efforts and Success Stories

Amidst the environmental challenges facing the world, there are numerous conservation efforts and success stories that highlight the potential for positive change and the importance of proactive conservation initiatives. These efforts, led by governments, non-governmental organizations (NGOs), local communities, and individuals, demonstrate the power of collective action in protecting and restoring ecosystems, conserving biodiversity, and promoting sustainable development. Here are some notable examples of conservation efforts and success stories from around the world:

1. **Galápagos Islands, Ecuador:**
   The Galápagos Islands, renowned for their unique biodiversity and evolutionary significance, have benefited from decades of conservation efforts aimed at preserving their fragile ecosystems. Strict regulations, protected areas, and sustainable tourism practices have helped to safeguard iconic species such as giant tortoises, marine iguanas, and blue-footed boobies. The Galápagos National Park and Marine Reserve serve as models of effective conservation management and ecotourism.

2. **Panda Conservation, China:**
   The giant panda, an iconic symbol of wildlife conservation, has experienced a remarkable recovery in recent years thanks to intensive conservation efforts in China. Conservation measures such as habitat protection, captive breeding, and community engagement have contributed to an increase in the panda population and the expansion of its range. The success of panda conservation efforts underscores the importance of habitat preservation and species recovery programs.

3. **Yellowstone National Park, USA:**
   Yellowstone National Park, America's first national park, is celebrated for its natural beauty, biodiversity, and ecological restoration efforts. Conservation initiatives such as the reintroduction of wolves and bison, the restoration of riparian habitats, and the management of invasive species have helped to restore balance to the park's ecosystems and enhance its resilience to climate change. Yellowstone serves as a living laboratory for conservation research and a model for protected area management worldwide.

4. **Community-Based Conservation, Namibia:**
   Namibia's community-based conservation programs empower local communities to manage and benefit from their natural resources sustainably. Initiatives such as communal conservancies, wildlife conservancies, and community-owned lodges enable rural communities to generate income from ecotourism, trophy hunting, and other conservation activities while conserving wildlife habitats and reducing human-wildlife conflicts. These initiatives have contributed to the recovery of wildlife populations and the conservation of vast wilderness areas.

5. Great Barrier Reef, Australia:
   The Great Barrier Reef, the world's largest coral reef system, faces numerous threats including climate change, coral bleaching, and pollution. Conservation efforts such as marine protected areas, coral reef monitoring programs, and reef restoration projects aim to protect and restore the reef's biodiversity and ecological resilience. Collaborative efforts between government agencies, researchers, NGOs, and local communities are essential for safeguarding the Great Barrier Reef for future generations.

6. Tree Planting Initiatives, Global:
   Tree planting initiatives around the world are combating deforestation, mitigating climate change, and restoring degraded landscapes. Projects such as the Great Green Wall in Africa, the Billion Tree Campaign, and national reforestation programs are planting millions of trees to restore forests, combat desertification, and provide ecosystem services such as carbon sequestration, soil conservation, and habitat restoration. These efforts demonstrate the potential for nature-based solutions to address environmental challenges.

Environmental Activism Around the Globe

Environmental activism plays a crucial role in raising awareness, advocating for policy changes, and mobilizing action to address global environmental challenges. From grassroots movements to international campaigns, environmental activists around the world are working tirelessly to protect ecosystems, combat climate change, and promote sustainability. Here are some examples of environmental activism from different regions:

1. Youth Climate Strikes:
   Inspired by Swedish activist Greta Thunberg, youth-led climate strikes and protests have swept across the globe, with students from countries worldwide demanding urgent action on climate change. These movements, such as Fridays for Future, have galvanized millions of young people to take to the streets, call for stronger climate policies, and hold governments and corporations accountable for their environmental actions.

2. Indigenous Rights and Land Defense:

Indigenous communities are at the forefront of environmental activism, defending their traditional lands, territories, and natural resources from exploitation and destruction. From the Standing Rock Sioux Tribe's opposition to the Dakota Access Pipeline in the United States to the struggles of indigenous peoples in the Amazon rainforest against deforestation and mining, indigenous-led movements highlight the link between environmental conservation and human rights.

3. Anti-Deforestation Campaigns:

Deforestation is a major environmental issue globally, particularly in regions such as the Amazon, Congo Basin, and Southeast Asia. Environmental activists and organizations are campaigning against deforestation by raising awareness about its impacts on biodiversity, climate change, and local communities. Campaigns to protect forests often involve advocacy, legal action, and grassroots mobilization to pressure governments and corporations to halt deforestation and promote sustainable land use practices.

4. Plastic Pollution Awareness:

The proliferation of plastic pollution in oceans, rivers, and landscapes has sparked widespread concern and activism around the world. Environmental organizations, community groups, and individuals are raising awareness about the harmful effects of plastic pollution on marine life, ecosystems, and human health. Campaigns to reduce single-use plastics, promote recycling, and clean up plastic waste are mobilizing citizens and driving policy changes at local, national, and international levels.

5. Climate Litigation:

Climate litigation has emerged as a powerful tool for holding governments and corporations accountable for their role in climate change. Activist groups, NGOs, and individuals are filing lawsuits against governments and fossil fuel companies for failing to take adequate action to address climate change and protect human rights. These legal battles seek to compel policymakers and polluters to reduce greenhouse gas emissions, transition to renewable energy, and mitigate the impacts of climate change on vulnerable communities.

6. **Global Climate Summits and Conferences:**
   International climate summits and conferences, such as the United Nations Climate Change Conferences (COP), provide platforms for environmental activists, scientists, policymakers, and civil society organizations to come together to discuss climate action and negotiate global agreements. These events serve as focal points for environmental activism, mobilizing public support for ambitious climate goals and holding governments accountable for their commitments under international agreements such as the Paris Agreement.

The Role of Indigenous Communities in Conservation

Indigenous communities around the world have long been stewards of their lands, possessing traditional knowledge and sustainable practices that contribute to biodiversity conservation, ecosystem management, and environmental resilience. Their holistic approach to conservation emphasizes the interconnectedness of humans, nature, and culture, providing valuable insights and lessons for addressing global environmental challenges. Here are some key aspects of the role of indigenous communities in conservation:

1. **Traditional Ecological Knowledge (TEK):**
   Indigenous communities possess deep knowledge of their local ecosystems, including plants, animals, weather patterns, and ecological processes, accumulated over generations through observation, experience, and cultural practices. This traditional ecological knowledge (TEK) forms the basis for sustainable land management, resource use, and conservation strategies tailored to local conditions and needs.

2. **Sustainable Land Management Practices:**
   Indigenous peoples have developed sustainable land management practices that prioritize ecosystem health, biodiversity conservation, and cultural integrity. These practices, such as rotational agriculture, agroforestry, and community-based resource management, promote

resilience to environmental change, maintain soil fertility, and enhance biodiversity while ensuring the well-being of present and future generations.

3. Cultural and Spiritual Values:

Indigenous cultures often have deep spiritual and cultural connections to the land, viewing nature as sacred and worthy of reverence and respect. These cultural values motivate stewardship and conservation efforts, instilling a sense of responsibility and reciprocity towards the natural world and fostering harmonious relationships between humans and the environment.

4. Community-Based Conservation:

Indigenous communities play a central role in community-based conservation initiatives that empower local people to manage and protect their traditional territories. These initiatives, often led by indigenous organizations and supported by partnerships with NGOs, governments, and researchers, promote indigenous rights, self-determination, and sustainable development while conserving biodiversity and ecosystems.

5. Guardians of Biodiversity Hotspots:

Many indigenous territories overlap with globally significant biodiversity hotspots, including tropical rainforests, coral reefs, and Arctic ecosystems. Indigenous peoples act as guardians of these biodiversity hotspots, defending them against threats such as deforestation, habitat loss, illegal logging, and extractive industries. Their traditional territories serve as vital refuges for endangered species and critical habitats for ecosystem conservation.

6. Advocacy and Leadership:

Indigenous leaders and activists advocate for indigenous rights, environmental justice, and the recognition of indigenous knowledge and governance systems in conservation policies and practices. They participate in international forums, conferences, and campaigns to raise awareness about the role of indigenous peoples in conservation and to promote inclusive and equitable approaches to environmental governance.

7. **Climate Change Adaptation and Resilience:**
Indigenous communities are on the front lines of climate change, facing impacts such as changing weather patterns, loss of traditional livelihoods, and threats to cultural heritage. Indigenous knowledge and adaptation strategies, including traditional farming techniques, water management systems, and community-based early warning systems, contribute to climate resilience and adaptation efforts.

8. **Partnerships and Collaboration:**
Recognizing the value of indigenous knowledge and stewardship, governments, NGOs, and researchers increasingly engage in partnerships and collaborations with indigenous communities in conservation initiatives. These partnerships foster mutual learning, respect indigenous rights and sovereignty, and promote shared goals of biodiversity conservation, sustainable development, and cultural preservation.

Innovative Solutions to Environmental Problems

Addressing global environmental challenges requires creative thinking, technological innovation, and collaboration across sectors. From renewable energy and sustainable agriculture to waste management and conservation technology, numerous innovative solutions are emerging to mitigate environmental degradation, promote sustainability, and build resilience to climate change. Here are some examples of innovative solutions to environmental problems:

1. **Renewable Energy Technologies:**
Transitioning from fossil fuels to renewable energy sources such as solar, wind, and hydroelectric power is key to reducing greenhouse gas emissions and combating climate change. Innovative technologies such as floating solar farms, offshore wind turbines, and concentrated solar power systems are expanding renewable energy capacity and increasing energy efficiency, making clean energy more accessible and affordable.

2. **Green Building Design:**
Green building design incorporates sustainable materials, energy-efficient systems, and passive design strategies to minimize

environmental impact and maximize resource efficiency. Innovations such as green roofs, solar panels, rainwater harvesting, and natural ventilation systems are transforming the construction industry and promoting energy-efficient, environmentally friendly buildings and infrastructure.

3. Circular Economy Practices:
The circular economy aims to eliminate waste and promote resource efficiency by designing products, materials, and systems that can be reused, recycled, or repurposed at the end of their life cycle. Innovations such as product redesign, closed-loop recycling, and waste-to-energy technologies are closing the loop on resource consumption and waste generation, reducing pressure on natural ecosystems and fostering sustainable consumption and production patterns.

4. Precision Agriculture:
Precision agriculture uses advanced technologies such as drones, sensors, and data analytics to optimize farming practices, increase crop yields, and reduce environmental impacts. Innovations such as precision irrigation, smart farming equipment, and digital agriculture platforms enable farmers to monitor soil health, manage water usage, and minimize pesticide and fertilizer use, improving agricultural productivity while conserving resources and reducing emissions.

5. Nature-Based Solutions:
Nature-based solutions harness the power of ecosystems to address environmental challenges such as climate change, biodiversity loss, and natural disasters. Innovations such as reforestation, wetland restoration, and ecosystem-based adaptation strategies enhance ecosystem resilience, sequester carbon, and provide ecosystem services such as flood protection, water purification, and habitat restoration, contributing to sustainable development and climate resilience.

6. Biotechnology and Bioengineering:
Biotechnology and bioengineering offer innovative solutions to environmental problems, including pollution remediation, waste management, and sustainable resource utilization. Biotechnological innovations such as bioremediation, microbial fuel cells, and bio-based

materials enable the cleanup of contaminated sites, the conversion of waste into valuable resources, and the development of eco-friendly alternatives to conventional materials and chemicals.

7. Ocean Conservation Technologies:

Technologies such as autonomous underwater vehicles, satellite monitoring systems, and marine conservation drones are revolutionizing ocean conservation and management efforts. These innovations enable scientists, policymakers, and conservationists to monitor marine ecosystems, track marine species, and detect illegal fishing activities, supporting the protection and sustainable management of ocean resources and biodiversity.

8. Citizen Science and Community Engagement:

Citizen science initiatives empower individuals and communities to participate in environmental monitoring, data collection, and conservation efforts. Through smartphone apps, crowdsourcing platforms, and community science projects, citizens can contribute valuable data on biodiversity, air and water quality, and environmental changes, fostering public awareness, engagement, and stewardship of natural resources.

Chapter 18
Human Diversity and Cultural Exchange

The Beauty of Cultural Diversity

Cultural diversity is one of the most remarkable aspects of humanity, encompassing a rich tapestry of traditions, languages, beliefs, customs, and artistic expressions. It is a source of strength, resilience, and creativity, enriching societies and fostering understanding, tolerance, and mutual respect among people of different backgrounds. Here are some facets of the beauty of cultural diversity:

1. Unique Traditions and Customs:

Cultural diversity is manifested in the myriad of traditions and customs practiced by communities around the world. From festivals and ceremonies to rites of passage and daily rituals, each culture has its own unique way of celebrating, commemorating, and expressing shared values, beliefs, and experiences.

2. Language and Communication:

Language is a fundamental aspect of cultural identity and diversity, reflecting the unique history, worldview, and social dynamics of different communities. The world is home to thousands of languages, each with its own nuances, dialects, and expressions, connecting people to their cultural heritage and facilitating communication and expression.

3. Culinary Diversity:

Food is a universal language that transcends borders and bridges cultural divides. The diversity of cuisines around the world reflects the richness of cultural exchange, migration, and adaptation, with each dish telling a story of tradition, innovation, and regional flavors. Culinary diversity celebrates the art of cooking, sharing meals, and preserving culinary heritage.

4. Art, Music, and Dance:

Artistic expressions such as music, dance, literature, and visual arts are manifestations of cultural diversity, reflecting the creativity, imagination, and collective identity of societies. Traditional music and dance forms, folk tales and myths, and indigenous art forms showcase the beauty and diversity of human creativity and expression.

5. Architecture and Design:

Architectural styles, building techniques, and design aesthetics vary across cultures, reflecting local climate, geography, materials, and cultural values. From ancient monuments and historic landmarks to contemporary structures and urban landscapes, architectural diversity reflects the ingenuity, craftsmanship, and cultural identity of communities.

6. Spirituality and Belief Systems:

Cultural diversity is evident in the multitude of spiritual beliefs, religions, and philosophical traditions practiced worldwide. Each faith tradition offers its own perspective on the meaning of life, ethics, morality, and the human relationship to the divine, inspiring rituals, symbols, and practices that shape individual and collective identities.

7. Traditional Clothing and Textiles:

Traditional clothing and textiles reflect the cultural identity, social status, and aesthetic sensibilities of different communities. From intricate embroidery and vibrant patterns to symbolic motifs and traditional garments, textile traditions showcase the craftsmanship, creativity, and cultural heritage of societies.

8. Intercultural Exchange and Fusion:

Cultural diversity is dynamic and evolving, shaped by historical migration, trade, conquest, and intercultural exchange. As people interact and share ideas, traditions, and practices, cultures merge, adapt, and transform, giving rise to new forms of expression, hybrid identities, and multicultural societies.

Celebrating Multiculturalism and Inclusivity

Multiculturalism and inclusivity are essential principles that promote respect, understanding, and appreciation for the diverse identities, backgrounds, and experiences of individuals and communities around the world. Embracing multiculturalism enriches societies, fosters social cohesion, and creates opportunities for dialogue, collaboration, and mutual learning. Here are some ways in which multiculturalism and inclusivity are celebrated:

1. **Cultural Festivals and Events:**
Multicultural festivals and events celebrate the diverse traditions, cuisines, music, dance, and arts of different cultures, inviting people of all backgrounds to come together in celebration and solidarity. These events provide platforms for cultural exchange, intercultural dialogue, and community building, promoting cross-cultural understanding and appreciation.

2. **Diversity Awareness Campaigns:**
Diversity awareness campaigns raise awareness about the importance of embracing diversity, challenging stereotypes, and promoting inclusivity in all aspects of society. These campaigns encourage individuals and organizations to recognize and celebrate the unique contributions of people from diverse backgrounds and to create inclusive environments that welcome and respect everyone.

3. **Language and Cultural Exchange Programs:**
Language and cultural exchange programs facilitate cross-cultural learning and dialogue by bringing together people from different countries, cultures, and linguistic backgrounds. These programs provide opportunities for individuals to immerse themselves in new cultures, learn languages, and build friendships across cultural boundaries, fostering empathy, tolerance, and global citizenship.

4. **Inclusive Education and Curriculum:**
Inclusive education ensures that educational curricula, materials, and teaching practices reflect the diversity of students' backgrounds, experiences, and identities. Schools and educational institutions promote multiculturalism by incorporating diverse perspectives, histories, and cultural artifacts into their curricula, fostering critical thinking, empathy, and respect for cultural differences.

5. **Diverse Representation in Media and Arts:**
Representation matters in media, arts, and entertainment, as diverse and authentic portrayals of people from different backgrounds promote inclusivity and challenge stereotypes. Multiculturalism is celebrated through diverse storytelling, diverse casting, and platforms that

amplify the voices and experiences of marginalized communities, promoting empathy, understanding, and social change.

6. Interfaith Dialogue and Collaboration:

Interfaith dialogue and collaboration bring together people from different religious and spiritual traditions to promote understanding, respect, and cooperation. Multifaith initiatives and interfaith dialogue forums provide opportunities for individuals and communities to learn about and engage with diverse religious beliefs, practices, and perspectives, fostering religious pluralism and social cohesion.

7. Community Engagement and Integration:

Multicultural communities promote social integration and cohesion by providing support, resources, and services to newcomers and immigrants, facilitating their integration into society and promoting cross-cultural exchange and interaction. Community organizations, cultural centers, and immigrant support networks offer opportunities for individuals to connect, share experiences, and build inclusive communities.

8. Policy and Advocacy for Diversity and Inclusion:

Governments, policymakers, and advocacy groups play a critical role in promoting multiculturalism and inclusivity through policies, legislation, and advocacy efforts that combat discrimination, promote equal rights and opportunities, and create inclusive environments for all. Multiculturalism is celebrated through affirmative action policies, anti-discrimination laws, and initiatives that promote diversity and inclusion in employment, education, and public life.

Cross-Cultural Exchange Programs and Initiatives

Cross-cultural exchange programs and initiatives play a crucial role in fostering understanding, appreciation, and cooperation among people from diverse backgrounds. These programs provide opportunities for individuals to immerse themselves in new cultures, learn about different perspectives, and build connections across cultural boundaries. Here are some examples of cross-cultural exchange programs and initiatives:

1. Student Exchange Programs:

Student exchange programs enable students to study abroad or participate in cultural immersion programs in foreign countries. These programs provide opportunities for students to experience different educational systems, languages, and cultures, fostering intercultural understanding, language proficiency, and global citizenship.

2. Volunteer Abroad Programs:

Volunteer abroad programs allow individuals to contribute to community development projects, environmental conservation efforts, and humanitarian initiatives in foreign countries. Participants work alongside local communities, gaining firsthand experience of different cultures, lifestyles, and challenges while making a positive impact through service and collaboration.

3. Internship and Work Exchange Programs:

Internship and work exchange programs offer opportunities for individuals to gain professional experience, skills, and cultural insights by working or interning in foreign countries. Participants engage in cross-cultural workplaces, collaborate with colleagues from diverse backgrounds, and learn about different business practices, industries, and work cultures.

4. Cultural Immersion and Language Learning Programs:

Cultural immersion and language learning programs provide intensive language instruction, cultural activities, and homestay experiences in foreign countries. Participants immerse themselves in the language, customs, and daily life of the host culture, enhancing their language skills, cultural competence, and intercultural communication abilities.

5. International Research and Academic Collaboration:

International research and academic collaboration initiatives facilitate collaboration and knowledge exchange among scholars, scientists, and researchers from different countries and disciplines. These collaborations promote interdisciplinary research, cross-cultural dialogue, and the sharing of expertise, resources, and best practices to address global challenges.

6. Cultural Exchange Tours and Performances:

Cultural exchange tours, festivals, and performances bring together artists, musicians, dancers, and performers from different cultures to showcase their traditions, music, dance, and artistic expressions. These events promote cultural understanding, appreciation, and dialogue, fostering connections and shared experiences among audiences worldwide.

7. Professional and Leadership Development Programs:

Professional and leadership development programs offer training, workshops, and networking opportunities for emerging leaders, entrepreneurs, and professionals from diverse backgrounds. Participants engage in skill-building activities, mentorship programs, and cultural exchanges, gaining insights into global issues, leadership practices, and cross-cultural collaboration.

8. Virtual Exchange and Online Learning Platforms:

Virtual exchange and online learning platforms leverage technology to connect learners and educators from around the world, facilitating cross-cultural dialogue, collaboration, and learning. These platforms offer virtual classrooms, language exchange programs, and online courses that enable participants to interact, share ideas, and learn from each other regardless of geographic location.

Cultural Heritage Preservation Efforts

Cultural heritage preservation efforts are vital for safeguarding the rich diversity of human traditions, practices, artifacts, and expressions for present and future generations. These efforts aim to protect, conserve, and promote cultural heritage sites, monuments, artifacts, languages, and intangible cultural practices that hold significance for communities worldwide. Here are some key aspects of cultural heritage preservation efforts:

1. Conservation of Historic Sites and Monuments:

Cultural heritage sites and monuments, including ancient ruins, historic buildings, and archaeological sites, are vulnerable to natural disasters, environmental degradation, urbanization, and human activities. Preservation efforts involve conservation, restoration, and maintenance activities to protect these sites' integrity, authenticity, and cultural significance, ensuring they remain accessible and well-preserved for future generations.

2. Documentation and Digitization:

Documentation and digitization initiatives record, document, and archive cultural heritage artifacts, monuments, and traditions using digital technologies such as 3D scanning, photography, and digitization. These efforts create digital repositories, databases, and archives that preserve and disseminate cultural heritage materials, making them accessible to researchers, educators, and the public while safeguarding them from loss, damage, or destruction.

3. Intangible Cultural Heritage Preservation:

Intangible cultural heritage encompasses traditions, rituals, folklore, music, dance, oral traditions, and knowledge systems passed down through generations. Preservation efforts focus on safeguarding intangible cultural heritage practices from extinction, promoting their transmission, revitalization, and safeguarding through community-based initiatives, documentation, education, and awareness-raising activities.

4. Language Preservation and Revitalization:

Languages are essential carriers of cultural identity, knowledge, and heritage, yet many indigenous and minority languages are endangered or at risk of extinction due to globalization, urbanization, and language shift. Language preservation efforts involve documenting, revitalizing, and promoting endangered languages through language revitalization programs, literacy campaigns, language immersion schools, and community language projects.

5. Cultural Heritage Legislation and Policies:

Cultural heritage legislation and policies play a crucial role in protecting and preserving cultural heritage resources, ensuring their sustainable management, and preventing illicit trafficking, looting, and destruction of cultural artifacts and sites. Governments, international organizations, and heritage agencies enact laws, regulations, and conventions to safeguard cultural heritage and promote its sustainable development.

6. Community Engagement and Empowerment:

Community engagement and empowerment are central to cultural heritage preservation efforts, as local communities often hold deep knowledge, expertise, and attachment to their cultural heritage. Participatory approaches involve engaging communities in decision-making processes, planning, and management of cultural heritage sites and resources, fostering ownership, pride, and stewardship of their cultural heritage.

7. Capacity Building and Training:

Capacity building and training initiatives provide heritage professionals, educators, and community members with the skills, knowledge, and resources needed to undertake cultural heritage preservation activities effectively. Training programs cover topics such as conservation techniques, documentation methods, community-based heritage management, and sustainable tourism practices, building local capacity for heritage preservation and management.

8. Tourism and Sustainable Development:

Cultural heritage preservation contributes to sustainable development by promoting heritage tourism, sustainable tourism practices, and cultural heritage-based livelihoods that benefit local communities economically, socially, and environmentally. Sustainable tourism initiatives aim to minimize the negative impacts of tourism on cultural heritage sites while maximizing benefits for local communities and promoting responsible tourism practices.

Global Citizenship and Unity in Diversity

Global citizenship refers to the idea that individuals have a sense of belonging to a broader community beyond national or cultural boundaries, recognizing their interconnectedness with people worldwide and their shared responsibility for addressing global challenges. Unity in diversity embodies the notion that despite the differences in cultures, languages, religions, and beliefs, there is a common humanity that unites people across the globe. Here are some key aspects of global citizenship and unity in diversity:

1. Recognition of Shared Humanity:
Global citizenship emphasizes the recognition of the inherent dignity, rights, and worth of all individuals, irrespective of their nationality, ethnicity, religion, or socioeconomic status. It promotes empathy, compassion, and solidarity with people facing adversity and injustice, fostering a sense of collective responsibility for promoting human rights, equality, and social justice worldwide.

2. Respect for Cultural Diversity:
Unity in diversity celebrates the richness and diversity of human cultures, languages, traditions, and beliefs as sources of strength, resilience, and creativity. It promotes respect, tolerance, and understanding for cultural differences, encouraging dialogue, collaboration, and mutual learning among people from diverse backgrounds.

3. Promotion of Intercultural Understanding:
Global citizenship fosters intercultural understanding, communication, and cooperation across cultural and geographic boundaries. It encourages individuals to engage with diverse perspectives, challenge stereotypes, and build bridges of empathy and respect, promoting peaceful coexistence and harmony in multicultural societies.

4. Cross-Cultural Collaboration and Exchange:
Unity in diversity encourages cross-cultural collaboration, exchange, and partnership among individuals, communities, and organizations worldwide. It promotes dialogue, cooperation, and joint action on shared global challenges such as climate change, poverty, inequality, and conflict, harnessing the collective wisdom, resources, and creativity of diverse stakeholders.

5. Environmental Stewardship and Sustainability:
Global citizenship emphasizes the importance of environmental stewardship, sustainability, and the protection of the planet's ecosystems for current and future generations. It promotes awareness,

education, and action on environmental issues, encouraging individuals to adopt sustainable lifestyles, advocate for environmental conservation, and support efforts to address climate change and biodiversity loss.

6. Promotion of Peace and Conflict Resolution:

Unity in diversity promotes peaceful coexistence, dialogue, and conflict resolution as essential foundations for building a more just, equitable, and peaceful world. Global citizenship fosters understanding, empathy, and dialogue among people of different backgrounds, promoting non-violent approaches to resolving conflicts and addressing root causes of violence and injustice.

7. Advocacy for Social Justice and Equity:

Global citizenship advocates for social justice, equity, and inclusive development, challenging inequalities, discrimination, and systemic barriers that limit opportunities and hinder human flourishing. It promotes advocacy, activism, and civic engagement to advance the rights and well-being of marginalized and vulnerable populations, fostering a more just and equitable world for all.

8. Education for Global Citizenship:

Education plays a crucial role in fostering global citizenship by equipping individuals with the knowledge, skills, and values needed to engage as responsible and active global citizens. Global citizenship education promotes critical thinking, empathy, intercultural competence, and ethical leadership, empowering individuals to contribute positively to local and global communities.

Chapter 19
Uncommon Traditions and Superstitions

Unique Superstitions from Different Cultures

Superstitions are beliefs or practices that are based on irrational or supernatural assumptions, often passed down through generations within a particular culture or community. While some superstitions may seem peculiar or nonsensical to outsiders, they hold significant cultural and historical significance for those who adhere to them. Here are some unique superstitions from different cultures around the world:

1. **Breaking a Mirror (Western Culture):**
   In Western cultures, breaking a mirror is believed to bring seven years of bad luck. This superstition likely originated from ancient beliefs that mirrors were portals to the soul, and breaking one would cause harm to the soul.

2. **Seeing a Black Cat (Various Cultures):**
   Black cats have been associated with superstitions in various cultures. In Western cultures, it is often considered unlucky to cross paths with a black cat, especially if it crosses your path from left to right. However, in some cultures, such as Japanese and Scottish folklore, black cats are considered symbols of good luck.

3. **Opening an Umbrella Indoors (Various Cultures):**
   Many cultures have superstitions about opening an umbrella indoors, believing it will bring bad luck. This superstition may have originated from the idea that opening an umbrella indoors would offend the spirits or gods, or disrupt the natural order of the universe.

4. **Knocking on Wood (Western and Middle Eastern Cultures):**
   Knocking on wood is a superstition believed to ward off bad luck or prevent a jinx. It is common in Western cultures to knock on wood after making a statement to avoid tempting fate. A similar superstition exists in Middle Eastern cultures, where people may knock on wood or use other gestures to ward off the evil eye.

5. **Whistling at Night (Various Cultures):**
   Whistling at night is considered unlucky or inviting misfortune in many cultures. Some believe that whistling at night attracts evil spirits

or disturbs the peace of the night, while others associate it with inviting bad luck or supernatural occurrences.

6. Shoes on the Table (British and American Folklore):
Placing shoes on a table is considered unlucky in British and American folklore. This superstition may have originated from the belief that shoes on a table bring death or misfortune, as shoes are associated with the ground and should not be elevated to a place of importance.

7. Eating Grapes at Midnight (Spanish and Latin American Tradition):
In Spanish and Latin American cultures, it is a New Year's tradition to eat twelve grapes at midnight, one for each stroke of the clock. Each grape represents a wish for the coming year, and it is believed that eating the grapes will bring good luck and prosperity.

8. Bird Droppings (Various Cultures):
Bird droppings are often considered symbols of good luck in some cultures, especially if they land on a person or their belongings. In Japanese culture, for example, it is believed that being hit by bird droppings is a sign of good fortune and prosperity.

Rituals for Good Luck and Prosperity

Throughout history and across cultures, people have developed various rituals and practices believed to attract good luck, fortune, and prosperity into their lives. These rituals often involve symbolic actions, gestures, or objects that are believed to possess auspicious qualities or attract positive energies. Here are some examples of rituals for good luck and prosperity from different cultures:

1. Lucky Charms and Amulets:
Many cultures believe in the power of lucky charms and amulets to bring good fortune and protect against evil spirits or misfortune. These charms can take various forms, such as horseshoes, four-leaf clovers, lucky coins, and religious symbols like the evil eye or the Hamsa hand.

2. New Year's Traditions:

New Year's celebrations often include rituals and customs believed to usher in good luck and prosperity for the coming year. For example, in some cultures, people eat specific foods thought to bring abundance and prosperity, such as lentils (Italy), grapes (Spain), and fish (China).

3. Money Rituals:

Many cultures have rituals and traditions aimed at attracting wealth and financial prosperity. These rituals may involve actions such as placing coins or bills in specific locations within the home, burning certain herbs or incense, or performing prayers or chants focused on abundance and prosperity.

4. Feng Shui Practices:

Feng Shui, an ancient Chinese practice, emphasizes the arrangement of space and objects to harmonize energy flow and promote positive chi (life force energy). Practitioners of Feng Shui use various techniques, such as arranging furniture, using specific colors, and incorporating auspicious symbols, to enhance prosperity and well-being.

5. Incense and Smudging:

Burning incense or smudging with sacred herbs, such as sage or palo santo, is a common ritual in many cultures believed to cleanse negative energies and attract positive vibrations. This practice is often performed during auspicious occasions or to purify spaces and invite good luck and prosperity.

6. Lunar New Year Rituals:

Lunar New Year celebrations in Asian cultures often involve elaborate rituals and customs aimed at attracting good fortune and prosperity for the year ahead. These rituals may include offerings to ancestors, fireworks displays to ward off evil spirits, and symbolic gestures such as giving red envelopes filled with money.

7. Planting Seeds or Trees:

Planting seeds or trees is a symbolic ritual in many cultures associated with growth, abundance, and prosperity. Some cultures believe that planting a tree or sowing seeds on auspicious occasions, such as weddings or birthdays, will bring good luck and prosperity to the individual or family.

8. Wishing Wells and Sacred Waters:

Wishing wells and sacred water sources are often associated with rituals for good luck and prosperity. People may toss coins into a wishing well or bathe in sacred waters, such as hot springs or natural springs, believing that the water's healing properties will bring blessings and prosperity.

Uncommon Cultural Practices and Beliefs

Cultural practices and beliefs vary widely across different societies and regions, often reflecting unique historical, social, and environmental contexts. While some customs and traditions are well-known and widely practiced, others may be less familiar and considered uncommon or even peculiar by outsiders. Here are some examples of uncommon cultural practices and beliefs from around the world:

1. Finger Cutting Ceremony (Dani Tribe, Indonesia):

The Dani tribe of Papua, Indonesia, practices a ritual known as the "finger cutting ceremony" as a symbol of mourning and grief. During the ceremony, family members and relatives of the deceased cut off the tips of their fingers as a form of expression for the loss of a loved one. The practice is believed to appease ancestral spirits and demonstrate the depth of sorrow.

2. Crying Marriage (Tujia People, China):

In some regions of China, particularly among the Tujia ethnic group, brides are expected to participate in a ritual known as "crying marriage" before their wedding day. For one month prior to the wedding, the bride spends an hour each day crying, with her mother and other female relatives joining in. The practice is intended to express joy for the upcoming marriage while also symbolizing the bride's sadness at leaving her family.

3. Sky Burial (Tibet):

Sky burial, or "jha-tor," is a traditional Tibetan funeral practice in which the deceased's body is placed on a mountaintop to be exposed to the elements and scavenging birds, typically vultures. The practice is based on Buddhist beliefs in the impermanence of life and the cycle of death and rebirth. It is believed that the body's elements are returned to nature, and the soul is liberated to achieve enlightenment.

4. Baby Tossing (Solapur, India):

In the Indian city of Solapur, a unique ritual called "baby tossing" is practiced during the annual Hindu festival of Muharram. Babies are dropped from the roof of a shrine, falling around 50 feet, and caught by a group of men below. The ritual is believed to bring good luck and protection to the infants and is said to have been performed for over 500 years.

5. Bullet Ant Gloves (Satere-Mawe Tribe, Brazil):

As part of a rite of passage into manhood, young boys of the Satere-Mawe tribe in the Amazon rainforest undergo a ritual called "bullet ant gloves." The boys must wear gloves filled with bullet ants, whose stings are among the most painful in the world, for several minutes without showing signs of pain. The ritual is believed to impart strength and resilience to the boys.

6. Dung Spitting (Massai Tribe, Kenya and Tanzania):

Among the Massai tribe of Kenya and Tanzania, spitting is considered a form of blessing and protection. During traditional ceremonies and rituals, elders may bless individuals by spitting on them, often using saliva mixed with cow dung. The practice is believed to ward off evil spirits and bring good fortune.

7. Cow Parade (Various Cities Worldwide):

In several cities around the world, including Chicago, New York, and Prague, "cow parades" are held as unique public art events. Artists decorate life-size fiberglass cows with elaborate and often whimsical designs, which are then displayed in public spaces throughout the city. The cow parade tradition originated in Switzerland and has since spread to numerous cities globally.

8. Pillow Fight Day (Various Cities Worldwide):

International Pillow Fight Day is an annual event celebrated in cities around the world, where participants gather in public spaces to engage in mass pillow fights. The event, which typically takes place in April, is meant to promote joy, laughter, and community spirit, with participants of all ages joining in the fun.

Festivals Rooted in Superstitions

Festivals are an integral part of cultural traditions worldwide, often celebrating religious, seasonal, or historical events. Some festivals are deeply rooted in superstitions and beliefs, reflecting cultural practices aimed at warding off evil spirits, ensuring good fortune, or appeasing deities. Here are examples of festivals from around the world that have strong connections to superstitions:

1. **Hungry Ghost Festival (Various Asian Countries):**
   The Hungry Ghost Festival is celebrated in various Asian countries, including China, Taiwan, Malaysia, and Singapore. According to traditional beliefs, during the seventh month of the lunar calendar, the gates of hell are opened, allowing restless spirits to roam the earth. To appease these spirits and ensure good fortune, people perform rituals such as offering food, burning incense, and staging elaborate performances for the spirits.

2. **Diwali (India):**
   Diwali, also known as the Festival of Lights, is one of the most significant festivals in Hinduism, celebrated by millions of people across India and other countries with large Hindu populations. The festival signifies the victory of light over darkness and good over evil. To ward off evil spirits and attract prosperity, people light oil lamps, decorate their homes with colorful rangoli patterns, and burst firecrackers.

3. **Holi (India and Nepal):**
   Holi, known as the Festival of Colors, is celebrated primarily in India and Nepal to mark the arrival of spring. One of the main rituals of Holi involves throwing colored powders and water at each other, symbolizing the triumph of good over evil and the arrival of spring. It is

believed that the vibrant colors of Holi ward off evil spirits and bring good luck and prosperity.

4. Day of the Dead (Mexico):

Dia de los Muertos, or the Day of the Dead, is a Mexican holiday celebrated to honor deceased loved ones. During the festival, families create elaborate altars called ofrendas adorned with photos, candles, marigolds, and offerings of food and drink to welcome the spirits of the deceased back to the earthly realm. It is believed that by honoring and remembering the dead, their spirits will bring blessings and good fortune to the living.

5. Obon Festival (Japan):

Obon is a Buddhist festival celebrated in Japan to honor the spirits of ancestors. During the festival, families gather to clean and decorate graves, light lanterns, and perform traditional dances called Bon-Odori to welcome the spirits back to the earthly realm. It is believed that by honoring ancestors, their spirits will protect and bring blessings to the living.

6. Mid-Autumn Festival (China):

The Mid-Autumn Festival, also known as the Mooncake Festival, is celebrated in China and other East Asian countries to give thanks for the harvest and celebrate the full moon. One of the main customs of the festival is the consumption of mooncakes, round pastries filled with sweet fillings, symbolizing reunion and good fortune.

7. Lunar New Year (Various Asian Countries):

Lunar New Year, also known as Chinese New Year, is celebrated in various Asian countries, including China, Vietnam, and Korea, to mark the beginning of the lunar calendar. The festival is associated with numerous superstitions and rituals aimed at ensuring good luck and prosperity for the coming year, such as cleaning the house to sweep away bad luck, wearing red clothing for good fortune, and giving red envelopes filled with money to children.

The Influence of Superstitions on Daily Life

Superstitions have long played a significant role in shaping human behavior, beliefs, and cultural practices. Despite advances in science and technology, superstitions continue to influence daily life in various ways, affecting people's decisions, rituals, and interactions with the world around them. Here are some examples of how superstitions influence daily life:

1. Avoiding Unlucky Numbers and Dates:
Many people avoid certain numbers or dates believed to bring bad luck. For example, in Western cultures, the number 13 is often considered unlucky, leading to the avoidance of buildings or floors numbered 13 and the reluctance to undertake significant activities on Friday the 13th. Similarly, in some Asian cultures, the number 4 is associated with death and is considered highly unlucky.

2. Engaging in Superstitious Practices for Good Luck:
People often engage in superstitious practices in the hope of attracting good luck or avoiding misfortune. This may include wearing lucky charms or talismans, such as a rabbit's foot or a horseshoe, carrying a lucky coin, or performing rituals believed to bring good fortune, such as tossing salt over one's shoulder or knocking on wood.

3. Seeking Guidance from Astrology and Divination:
Many people consult astrology, horoscopes, and divination practices such as tarot card readings, palmistry, or tea leaf reading for guidance in their daily lives. Believers may use these practices to make decisions about relationships, career choices, or major life events based on perceived astrological influences or signs from the universe.

4. Rituals for Warding Off Evil Spirits and Bad Luck:
Superstitious rituals aimed at warding off evil spirits or bad luck are common in many cultures. For example, people may perform rituals such as throwing salt over their shoulder, spitting, or making the sign of the cross to protect themselves from harm. Others may carry out cleansing rituals, such as burning sage or incense, to purify their homes or ward off negative energies.

5. Influencing Travel and Business Decisions:

Superstitions can influence decisions related to travel and business. For example, some people may avoid traveling on certain days or taking certain routes believed to be unlucky, while others may choose specific dates or times for important meetings or business transactions based on auspicious astrological alignments or cultural beliefs.

6. Observing Taboos and Cultural Norms:

Superstitions often give rise to taboos and cultural norms that govern behavior in various contexts. For example, in many cultures, there are taboos surrounding topics such as death, illness, or pregnancy, with specific rituals or behaviors prescribed to avoid attracting bad luck or negative outcomes.

7. Using Superstitions as Coping Mechanisms:

Superstitions can serve as coping mechanisms during times of uncertainty or stress. Believers may turn to superstitions for comfort or reassurance, believing that performing certain rituals or practices will bring them luck or protect them from harm in challenging situations.

8. Influencing Health and Well-being Practices:

Superstitions can influence health and well-being practices, with some people incorporating superstitious beliefs into their wellness routines. This may include wearing specific colors or clothing items believed to have healing properties, avoiding certain foods or activities on particular days, or seeking alternative healing modalities based on superstitions or cultural traditions.